Cooperative Games in Education

Building Community Without Competition, Pre-K–12

Written and illustrated by Suzanne Lyons

Foreword by Alfie Kohn

TEACHERS COLLEGE PRESS

TEACHERS COLLEGE | COLUMBIA UNIVERSITY
NEW YORK AND LONDON

Published by Teachers College Press,® 1234 Amsterdam Avenue, New York, NY 10027

Front cover design by Rebecca Lown Design. Illustration by Suzanne Lyons.

Library of Congress Cataloging-in-Publication Data

Names: Lyons, Suzanne (Science teacher), author.
Title: Cooperative games in education : building community without competition, pre-K-12 / Suzanne Lyons.
Description: First. | New York, NY : Teachers College Press, 2022. | Includes bibliographical references and index. | Summary: "Cooperative Games in Education is the first comprehensive guide to the world of cooperative play and games for pre-K-12 learning. It includes a thorough pedagogical rationale and guidelines for practice, a survey of related research and scholarship, engaging anecdotes, illustrations, historical background, and an array of sample games to try. In cooperative games, players win or lose together, sharing the experience of fun and challenge. No one can be eliminated in a cooperative game. What is eliminated is us-versus-them perception and zero-sum thinking. When students come to see each other as allies, rather than rivals, there are profound interpersonal effects that enhance community, inclusion, and a positive classroom climate where all can learn and thrive. This accessible, lively resource explains the value of cooperative games with guidance to help teachers use them for maximum social-emotional and academic benefit. Cooperative Games in Education will also interest the broader community of administrators, therapists, school psychologists, game designers, child-care providers, and others who care for children and need tools that foster healthy development, positive relationships, and joy. Book Features: Discussion of relevant research and theory. Best practices for choosing and facilitating cooperative games, including how to integrate them into any curriculum, guide post-game reflection, and convert traditional competitive games to cooperative ones. A full chapter of educational cooperative games correlated to their educational purpose. Discussion of some of the most salient applications of cooperative games, such as social-emotional learning, academic subject-area instruction, cooperative learning, trauma-sensitive practice, bullying prevention, early childhood education, and more. User-friendly features such as questions for reflection, end-of-chapter games, charming author-generated illustrations, and classroom vignettes. A synthesis of interdisciplinary scholarship that includes the work of Montessori, Piaget, Froebel, and Dewey, as well as perspectives from neuroscience and evolutionary biology. The fascinating history of cooperative games, from their origin as a tool for peace education to their current role as a pop-culture entertainment phenomenon"—Provided by publisher.
Identifiers: LCCN 2021048638 (print) | LCCN 2021048639 (ebook) | ISBN 9780807766668 (paperback) | ISBN 9780807766675 (hardcover) | ISBN 9780807780886 (ebook)
Subjects: LCSH: Educational games. | Cooperative games (Mathematics) | Cooperation—Study and teaching.
Classification: LCC LB1029.G3 L96 2022 (print) | LCC LB1029.G3 (ebook) | DDC 371.33/7—dc23/eng/20211109
LC record available at https://lccn.loc.gov/2021048638
LC ebook record available at https://lccn.loc.gov/2021048639

ISBN 978-0-8077-6666-8 (paper)
ISBN 978-0-8077-6667-5 (hardcover)
ISBN 978-0-8077-8088-6 (ebook)

Printed on acid-free paper
Manufactured in the United States of America

This book is dedicated to
Anne Mijke van Harten,
founder of EarthGames.nl,
who introduced me to the world of cooperative games,
and walks the talk
of cooperation.

Contents

PART II. SOME COOPERATIVE GAMES AND
GUIDELINES FOR PRACTICE

Foreword

The reassuring bromide that "there's no such thing as a stupid question" can be easily refuted by spending a few minutes with a standardized test. But even if it were true, there is certainly such a thing as a depressing question. Over the course of my career, two stand out. The first was from a student after a talk I gave at his overachieving high school. "You're telling us not to just get in a race for the traditional rewards," he said. "But what else is there?"

The second question, which I've been asked more than once, was posed in each case after I made an offhand reference to cooperative games as a welcome alternative to the usual competitive kind. My questioner frowns, genuinely confused: "But how could it be a game if there aren't winners and losers?"

Team games require cooperation, of course, but we've come to assume that this just means the players on each team will work together in order to triumph over another group of people who are working together. In other words, cooperation is merely a means; victory is the end. This reality is experienced so continuously and pervasively in our society that children learn (without anyone's having to tell them) that playing fields are like battlefields; it's us against them. A game by definition, we're led to conclude, is a recreational event in which half the players must fail. Even physical activities pursued by individuals (rather than teams), which in theory could be just about doing well and/or having fun—running, swimming, skiing, weight-lifting, gymnastics—are gratuitously turned into adversarial affairs where it's me against everyone else.*

---

* In a truly pathological culture, competition metastasizes to non-physical pursuits so that students are pitted against each other even when they're, say, performing individually or singing together or designing experiments. Talent "shows," choral "festivals," and science "fairs" are all set up as competitions. It's the same when kids write poetry or computer code, when they show off their mastery of oratory, math, geography, or spelling—the unspoken rule is that all these things must take place in the context of a contest, such that the goal is to beat other kids who are doing the same thing. With team sports, of course, competition is baked in; to avoid it, football, baseball, basketball, hockey, and soccer would need to be replaced with different games. In a way it's even sadder that we impose competition on activities that *aren't* inherently competitive.

Now, if you've picked up this book, you already know that some games *don't* sort players into winners and losers—and are especially delightful precisely because everyone is working together toward the same goal. Only after you've had some experience with cooperative games do you fully grasp just how much fun competition *isn't*.

In its purest form, the point of play is that it has no point —no goal other than itself. Competitive play is thus a contradiction in terms. A strict definition of play also excludes rule-driven cooperative games, but they at least retain more of a playful spirit. Cooperative board games, like cooperative outdoor activities involving physical exertion, can be thoroughly enjoyable even as they provide challenge, build skills, and offer undiluted camaraderie (as opposed to the warped version that's contingent on defeating a common enemy). As Suzanne Lyons argues in the pages that follow, by setting up a scenario where everyone is rooting for everyone else, cooperative games teach children important lessons about the possibility, the practical benefits, and the deep satisfaction of doing things with, rather than against, other people.

Recreation isn't a self-enclosed arena; it is, willy-nilly, a socialization tool that prepares children for adult roles. If the recreation is competitive, then it offers a kind of apprenticeship for life in corporate capitalism, in which other people are regarded as potential obstacles to one's own success. Sports teach children to accept the value, and even the inevitability, of adversarial relationships in place of solidarity and collective effort. As the sociologist David Riesman memorably put it, "The road to the board room leads through the locker room."

We can shrug and treat those competitive norms and institutions as facts of life for which children must be prepared (by immersing them in competitive rituals while they're small). Or we can introduce them to something different. The latter option sends the message that it's possible to challenge, rather than just accommodate ourselves to, dysfunctional arrangements. It points out that competition is just such an arrangement, ripe for challenge. And it offers a notable example of how *structural* reform—a far more promising strategy than trying to alter the attitudes of millions of individuals—can happen right here and right now. "Structural" or "systemic" change doesn't always involve, and needn't wait for, wholesale social transformation.

"Better get used to it" is a common rationalization not only for subjecting children to competition but for the unfairness of having parents use their greater skill or strength to defeat their kids in competitive games. The alternative is to let the child win, which is patronizing and eventually becomes awkwardly obvious. But cooperative games neatly eliminate the dilemma: Not only is it fine for adults to do their best, but they can share strategies and teach negotiation while having a lot of fun. Lyons notes that cooperative games are also a perfect complement to cooperative learning, which is the default arrangement in outstanding classrooms from kindergarten through graduate school: students in pairs or small groups making sense of ideas together.

Some years ago, having accepted an invitation to speak at a conference for physical education teachers, I feared that after laying out the harms of competition I would need a bodyguard to leave the room in one piece. Amazingly, my message was warmly received, which reminded me that teaching physical education is a completely different line of work from coaching sports.

You can understand my apprehension, though. After all, the first game that many of us experienced is a prototype of artificial scarcity. It typically takes place at a birthday party, where x players must scramble for x-1 chairs every time the music stops. In each round a child is eliminated—*out! out! out!*—until at the end only one remains triumphantly seated while everyone else is left standing on the sidelines: excluded from play . . . unhappy . . . losers. That's how you're taught to have a good time in America.

To learn more about the wonderful alternative, turn the page.

—Alfie Kohn

Acknowledgments

This book, befitting its subject matter, has been a collaborative effort. There are many people to thank. First, I acknowledge the thinkers, teachers, and writers whose ideas on cooperation provide the foundation for this work. I begin with Alfie Kohn. If not for his bestseller of 30+ years ago, *No Contest, The Case Against Competition*, we could not understand the need for cooperative games so clearly today. His impeccable arguments have surely not just turned heads but also changed lives—and disrupted dubious educational practices nationwide. That he has taken the time to write an electrifying foreword is thus an amazing gift, which I thank him for. The ideas I delve into in these pages also derive from the writings of Terry Orlick, Nel Noddings, Arnold P. Goldstein, Theo Lentz and Ruth Cornelius, Elizabeth Cohen and Rachel Lotan, Diane Levin, David W. Johnson and Roger T. Johnson, Morton Deutsch, and Christopher Allen.

I appreciate Sarah Biondello, acquisitions editor at Teachers College Press, who understood from the outset why a book on cooperative games would be worthy in these times. Sarah's effort and moral support carried this book from aspiration to concrete reality. I gratefully acknowledge development editor Susan Liddicoat for numerous good ideas that have made the book easier and more pleasant to read. Thanks to managing editor Mike Olivo for guiding the manuscript through production, and to Emily Freyer and the whole marketing team for their skill with promotion. Kudos to the designers for creating a perfect cover. I appreciate them for trusting me to do the illustrations, too. Thank you, Teachers College Press!

I send gratitude to friends, allies, and colleagues who I have learned from and enjoyed working with on many educational projects. These include my *Conceptual Integrated Science* textbook co-authors Paul Hewitt, John Suchocki, and Jennifer Yeh. Their encouragement and sympatico mean so much. I thank Jim Deacove for his wit, sensitivity, and accessibility, and of course for his genius idea: cooperative board games. I appreciate Ken and Jan Kolsbun for teaching me how to run a small business dedicated to positive social change. I thank my cooperative games comrade, Anne Mijke van Harten, for getting me interested in cooperative games in the first place and for her continuing support. I thank children's advocate and troubadour

Raffi, along with Kim Layton and Bert Simpson, for collaborating with me on The Baby Beluga Game.

Finally, to my family, I send love and gratitude. My husband Pete Lang, my children Tristan and Arianna, and my sisters Francine and Caroline keep my days happy and full even in this challenging era. Their everyday care and companionship keep life bouncing along like an ongoing cooperative game. Thanks!

Introduction

What if there were a dessert—say, a flavor of ice cream—that not only tastes delicious but also makes you kinder, wiser, more productive, and happier? Imagine that this ice cream is also healthy in every way, so the more you eat, the better off you are. Further, it is free or inexpensive, available to everyone, great for the environment, and it fosters equity, unity, democracy, and world peace besides. Want some?

This book is about such a treat. It is not about an ice cream, but rather a way to play—*cooperatively*—through cooperative games. Cooperative games are about having fun together so that all can win, rather than competing so that only a few succeed.

ABOUT PLAYING TOGETHER

Who says winning must involve beating someone else? Unfortunately, most people we meet. Competition and individualism are longstanding ideals in American culture. Accordingly, here in the United States and in many other cultures, too, winning is conceived in individualistic and competitive terms. The schools reflect and reinforce this by emphasizing competition and individualism in a variety of ways throughout the school day (Kohn, 1986). But it need not be so. There is an entire genre of games built on a different paradigm. Cooperative games help us discover that it can be just as much fun—and perhaps more so—to play *with* each other rather than *against* each other. Cooperative games exist for all ages and settings. They range from field games to circle games to party games to board games to online games—and more.

In cooperative games, players cooperate rather than compete. Everyone wins—or loses—together. The outcome is either communal joy or reciprocal consolation with shared commitment to do better next time. Play is a team effort, with *all* players participating on the same side, and with one shared goal. This setup means that players interact as friends rather than rivals. Besides noncompetition, the other defining feature of cooperative games is non-elimination. No player is ever cast out mid-game. Everyone is included until the game is over.

1

All of this is directly opposite to the group dynamics of traditional competitive games. Competitive games are *zero-sum* games. That means that every win comes at the expense of someone else's loss. It's *me-against-you* and *us-against-them*. Cooperative games are not zero-sum. Rather, they are *win-win*. This is a complete paradigm shift.

The idea of cooperative games was expressed for the first time, as far as an exhaustive literature search can determine, in the work of peace educators Ruth Cornelius and Theo Lentz in the early 1950s. A short self-published manual, *All Together: A Manual of Cooperative Games*, proposes the concept, coins the term, offers games, and discusses their effects on schoolchildren (Cornelius & Lentz, 1950). This publication never received wide circulation, however. In the 1960s, the notion resurfaced in the work of Stuart Brand and other champions of the counterculture as "New Games." New Games were conceived to "create a new set of rules, and with them a new way to live," which would be based on peace, cooperation and empathy (Turner, 2006). In 1978, the idea of playing together, not against each other, took hold in a broader swath of the public when Terry Orlick published his seminal book *The Cooperative Sports and Games Book: Challenge Without Competition*. Cooperative board games also originated in the 1970s through the efforts of Jim Deacove, who founded the small manufacturer Family Pastimes in Canada (personal communication, January 21, 2021). Still, the concept of cooperative games remained relatively obscure for decades more. It did not break through in American popular culture until about 2010. That is when digital cooperative games and cooperative board games rose to fame and acclaim in the worldwide gaming community.

Despite the early wave of excitement among educators and the current popularity of cooperative games among gamers, cooperative games are not much discussed in educational circles at this time. There is little current research focused on them, they are not often a topic at educational conferences, they are not featured in teacher education courses, and there are few articles about them in the educational press.

In a world where competitive games and sports are still very much the norm, cooperative games may seem out of sync with the realities of schooling and culture. But once they are experienced, cooperative games are usually embraced enthusiastically. In fact, young children exposed to both game types have been shown to prefer cooperation (Kohn, 1986). Besides being accepted as fun, cooperative games bring about numerous social-psychological benefits. These benefits include teaching the vital skill of cooperation, increasing kindness, and reducing aggression, according to numerous studies (Goldstein, 2002; Orlick, 1981).

WHY THIS BOOK?

Audience

This book aims to present a comprehensive and up-to-date summary of the *why* and *how-to* of cooperative games in education. This includes a pedagogical rationale and practical classroom tips that will enable teachers to use the games effectively. In addition, this book is intended to serve educational leaders, administrators, and policy makers. Cooperative games are a versatile teaching tool that supports many educational goals, so it is clear that decision-makers should be better acquainted with their merits. Academic researchers can use this book for ideas, information, and references that support their own related studies. Parents and child-care providers will obtain guidance on positive ways to raise happy and healthy children. Honestly, just about everyone who likes to play, wants to have more fun connecting with people, and appreciates prosocial ways of living can benefit from knowing more about cooperative games.

Books are often written by people with knowledge they urgently want to convey, which is certainly the case with this book. My involvement in cooperative games dates back over a dozen years. I first heard about the concept through a colleague I met at an education conference in 2009. Anne Mijke van Harten is a social entrepreneur who founded the small business Earth Games in the Netherlands. She and I were both attending a *Sharing Nature with Children* conference in Nevada City, California, high up in the Sierras. I had just finished co-authoring the textbook *Conceptual Integrated Science*. I am a physics and earth science educator who deeply respects the role of fun in education. My mentor Paul Hewitt has been a huge influence. He revolutionized physics teaching with his joyful physics textbook *Conceptual Physics*, first published in the 1970s. The book broke through the dread associated with traditional physics instruction by weaving engaging cartoons and funny asides into the solid physics content. *Conceptual Physics* has been the most popular physics text in America for 50 years and remains so today! Paul's success is shining proof of the power of fun in learning.

But I was attending the conference because I had hit an obstacle. I realized that when it comes to teaching topics such as climate change and other environmental hazards, scientific information is not enough. I noticed that disturbing facts tend to impart a sense of fear and futility rather than the will to learn and act. I did not see a way to integrate the "secret sauce" of fun into this teaching, either. Enter cooperative games.

Anne Mijke showed me that cooperative games inherently make learning fun because they are games, after all. They breed active engagement rather than denial and defeat by creating a microcosm where students can problem-solve. They embody a can-do spirit. Further, they model collaboration and joint effort toward our common problems, which is so clearly the mode by which humanity must tackle our shared, global-scale environmental issues. Games such as Save the Whales by Ken Kolsbun showed that cooperative board games were already delighting, teaching, and motivating youth toward environmental action in the social circles where they were known. Inspired, I soon launched CooperativeGames.com.

Though science teaching was the impetus for CooperativeGames.com, I soon realized there is another major application in schooling: social-emotional learning (SEL). Many visitors to CooperativeGames.com were therapists or educational psychologists who used the games for play therapy. Angry children; shy or withdrawn children; frightened, distrustful, traumatized children; autistic children; bullies and the bullied—these children and their sad, hurt parents all needed the healing, gentle connection that cooperative play provides.

The therapists and educators coming to CooperativeGames.com shared stories of how the games had helped their clients. They also made me aware of research on the psychology of competition, cooperation, and cooperative play. It was eye-opening. The evidence was plain even if rarely discussed: *Cooperative games can measurably improve social skills and reduce aggression* (Bay-Hinitz, Peterson, & Quiltch, 1994; Goldstein, 2002). How profound!

Coincidentally, around the time that I was discovering the merits of cooperative play, my daughter was experiencing bullying at school. The ability of cooperative games to foster prosocial behavior and decrease aggression became personally relevant. I redoubled my commitment to investigate and advocate for cooperative games in education. Eventually, I would gather together research and information showing that the applications for cooperative games extend well beyond SEL and teaching science. As you read through these pages, you will see that cooperative games embody—and teach—a win-win paradigm of social interaction that addresses many of our widespread societal problems.

Although the brilliant idea of cooperative games seemed marginal in 2009, it soon became mainstream. Minecraft, a digital game, exemplifies the trend. Fully released 2009, it is now a global sensation with well over 100 million registered users (Thompson, 2016). The cooperative-play mode of Minecraft involves exploring a brightly colored virtual landscape, building fanciful structures, sharing creative ideas and technical know-how, meeting friends, and collaborating on construction projects (Stuart, 2019). The game Pandemic, created by Matt Leacock and published in 2008, was the first cooperative board game to achieve blockbuster sales. In Pandemic, participants play roles such as dispatcher, researcher, and quarantine specialist. They pool their resources and capabilities to beat deadly disease and save humanity. The COVID crisis has only magnified the prescient message of the board game. Escape rooms, also called *escape games*, represent the trend toward cooperation in entertainment as well. In an escape room, players cooperate to solve puzzles, complete tasks, and use clues to find their way out of a haunted house or other gamified physical space. "Co-op gaming" has become a regular part of growing up.

The time is right for peaceful, productive play to flourish in the schools on a wider scale than ever before. The timeliness of cooperative gaming for entertainment, combined with the early foundational work by educators and activists, sets the stage for teachers today.

CONTENTS OF THIS BOOK

This book encompasses guidelines for practice as well as the theory that justifies cooperative games for educational purposes. The classroom tips and techniques show how to choose good games with educational value, set them up, lead them, and hold postgame discussions. This is vital information, but the theory is just as essential. You may need to explain the purpose of cooperative games to curious colleagues or parents who wonder why in the world an alternative to competition is needed. If so, the theoretical arguments and research explained and cited here will help (see also Appendix B, "Resources for Further Exploration"). What and how you communicate about the games will shape students' experiences and what they take away. Your deep understanding of cooperative play will be the source of your own authentic voice, which is your true power to help and heal.

How is this book—your short course in cooperative games—organized? Part I includes three chapters that contain essential theory and background information. Chapter 1 discusses play in general, the role of play in learning, and the special place that cooperative games occupy in the pantheon of play. Chapter 2 explores the nature of cooperation, why it is so important to teach in school, and the value of using play to teach cooperation. Chapter 3 considers the rarely discussed hazards of competition in schooling. It will help you understand why cooperative games are needed as an alternative and counterbalance. Together, the chapters in Part I show how cooperative games relate to the fundamental purposes of education.

Part II is a book within a book. It is a teaching manual for hands-on practice that you can refer to again and again. In Chapter 4, I provide an array of different kinds of cooperative games so that you have a sense of available options. Chapter 5 begins with best practices for choosing and facilitating games. Then you will learn a bit about cooperative game design and how to convert traditional competitive games to cooperative ones, to round out Part II.

Chapters 6 through 9 in Part III discuss the theory and practice of some of the most salient applications of cooperative games, including preparation for cooperative learning, SEL, preventing aggression, trauma-sensitive practice, early childhood education, and more. The pedagogical rationales and implementation strategies for different applications vary. These chapters may surprise you. Cooperative games turn out to be very versatile. They are useful for many educational purposes.

Throughout Parts I, II, and III, special text features are used to enhance your reading experience. *Questions for Reflection* highlight concepts that merit extra consideration. Answers are provided in Appendix A. Each chapter also includes a *Chapter Summary* that you can use as a checklist of the chapter's major points. Finally, each chapter ends with the *Play to Learn* section. *Play to Learn* provides a sample game so that you, too, can learn experientially through play.

The book comes to a close with the Epilogue. The Epilogue synthesizes the relevant principles and guidelines to build a framework that encompasses it all. Use, share, and enjoy!

Part I

FOUNDATIONS OF COOPERATIVE GAMES

CHAPTER 1

What Are Cooperative Play and Games?

The more we get together, the happier we'll be.

—Traditional American Children's Song

> Christine was a well-balanced child, well-liked by many and liking many children. In playing cooperative games, Christine showed joy when others contributed to the success of the game. She often initiated a game and others came to join her. She was patient in teaching a game to others. Often when playing jacks, she would state the progress of the game if an adult passed near where they were playing. When the group succeeded at throwing sixes in jacks, Christine enthusiastically called out "We *won!*" If the game was lost, she was willing to try again. Others often followed her example and tried the game again.
>
> —Ruth Cornelius & Theo Lentz (1950)

UNDERSTANDING PLAY

Play is a great teacher. As Piaget, Vygotsky, and so many others have described, play is essential for healthy human development in all its facets: cognitive, social, emotional, physical, and even spiritual (F. Hughes, 2010). Play is so vital that the United Nations declared it a human right of children (United Nations Office of the High Commissioner on Human Rights, 1989). Play is especially vital to children, but adults need to partake too. Whether we recognize it or not, many adult experiences of fun and relaxation are forms of play. But what exactly *is* play?

Close examination shows that play has fuzzy boundaries. Still, social scientists have identified five elements that characterize it. Play is:

- *Intrinsically motivated.* In other words, we play because we have an internal drive to do so—not because it yields any external rewards. Its outcome does not matter beyond the game. Play is an end in itself.

- *Freely chosen.* Play is completely voluntary. If someone is forcing you to play, you are not really playing.
- *Pleasurable.* Play is typically fun, but the pleasure may consist of other kinds of positive affect such as excitement, amusement, or joy.
- *Detached from reality.* Play is nonliteral in the sense that it has imaginary elements. There is a sense of detachment from the "real world."
- *Actively engaged in.* The player is fully involved psychologically and perhaps physically too. Her state of mind is not passive or indifferent.

Putting the five essential elements together, we have a useful working definition of play based on social science: Play is an active, engaging, and voluntary activity that is nonliteral and produces feelings of well-being such as fun, joy, or contentment and where outcome does not matter beyond the game (Gray, 2008; F. Hughes, 2010).

We see that in the magical realm of play, the pressures of real life are forgotten. Players are able to take risks, mess about, and try new things. Their lack of concern about real consequences combined with active engagement, makes players anxiety-free and ready to learn.

Play can be distinguished as *solitary, competitive*, or *cooperative. Solitary play* includes a vast range of playful activities that individuals enjoy by themselves. Examples include drawing pictures, conversing with an imaginary friend, and playing solo card games such as Solitaire. By contrast, *competitive play* is social play based on the zero-sum paradigm. In competitive play, one player (or team) wins by defeating another. Chess, soccer, and Monopoly are examples. *Cooperative play* is social play that is devoid of competition. Playing "house," collaborating to build a tree fort, clapping and singing in unison, joining co-op games online, and walloping a piñata to spill treats for all to share are examples of cooperative play.

QUESTIONS FOR REFLECTION

1. Henry plays football because his parents want him to. He would rather spend his free time tinkering with mechanical things. On the football field, he feels anxious. He is afraid he will be judged a "loser." Is Henry playing when he participates in football?
2. Consuelo is happily making cupcakes for a party. Is she playing?
3. Is play a subjective experience? Explain your thinking.

Play is not an all-or-nothing proposition. A playful attitude can be brought to bear on real-world situations where outcome actually does matter. So, while play can exist in a pure form, playful states of being occur in circumstances that look more like work than play. A playful mindset goes a long way to creating a playful experience.

Games are a category of play. They typically involve meeting a challenge or accomplishing a goal. Games, by definition, have *rules*—explicit guidelines that constrain players' behavior.

DEFINING COOPERATIVE GAMES

Cooperative games are defined as games in which players cooperate with one another rather than compete. They are structured according to rules that assure that players work together toward a shared goal. The degree of collaboration varies among different games. In some games, players cooperate through intricate strategy. Other games involve looser, noncompetitive social interaction. Many cooperative games, particularly board games, immerse players in a story that relates to cooperation. The narrative might involve finding a cure for a plague as in Pandemic, saving whales as in Save the Whales, or rounding up horses as in Round-Up. In all cases, it is more fun to win—but losing is not so bad either, because the experience is shared. One rule pertains in all cooperative games: No one can be eliminated (Orlick, 2006). The no-elimination rule means that everybody wins or loses together. All are in the same boat, and no one can be cast overboard!

Cooperative games exist in virtually all game formats, including field games, circle games, board games, video games, online games, and more. Some require materials; many do not. Some cooperative games are old, some are new, and many are middle-aged—dating back to the cooperative-games movement of the later 20th century.

A BRIEF HISTORY OF COOPERATIVE GAMES

Origins Cooperatively structured play and games are actually traditional. People have been playing together in noncompetitive ways since time immemorial. The natural impulse to play in a noncompetitive fashion can be observed anytime young children build a sand castle, play "House," or join in classic "nursery school" games such as London Bridge Is Falling Down. Older children and adults play cooperatively when they work on a jigsaw puzzle together, play a game of charades, or toss a Frisbee. What is more new and notable than generic cooperative play and games is the *cooperative-games movement*. This movement made cooperative games an intentional form of play, distinguishable from competition-based play, and defined the term "cooperative game" in its modern sense.

The Cooperative-Games Movement As explained in the Introduction, the earliest expression of the cooperative-games movement can be found in a short booklet written by 1st-grade teacher Ruth Cornelius and education professor Theo Lentz (1950). Both Cornelius and Lentz were peace educators looking for ways to transform culture toward peace as a response to the horrors of World War II. The notion gained traction in the 1960s when antiwar activists including Stuart Brand experimented with alternatives to traditional competitive games (Turner, 2006).

In the 1970s, cooperative games caught on in a larger, more mainstream audience comprised mainly of socially conscious parents and educators. This critical step forward occurred largely through the efforts of Terry Orlick, a former kinesiology professor at the University of Ottawa, Canada, and an Olympic coach. He is the author of several groundbreaking research studies plus a handful of books on the subject. These include the widely read games manual *The Cooperative Sports and Games Book: Challenge Without Competition* (1978). A groundswell of excitement among educators led to considerable implementation and research on cooperative games during the late 1970s and 1980s. But the excitement waned as humanistic approaches faded in the 1990s with the rise of assessment-driven reforms (Goldstein, 2002).

The first-wave cooperative games movement accomplished much during its brief lifetime. It was the rich soil in which the concept of playing together for peace germinated and began to grow. It produced a sizable grassroots following. The early cooperative games movement also led to some serious scholarly inquiry and formal research that remains important today. The movement articulated the premise that cooperative games have important social and academic benefits and therefore have a legitimate role in education. Further, the early movement inspired the first cooperative games for entertainment, whose descendants are thriving today. And, of course, the movement led to a lot of people having a lot of fun.

The Current State of Cooperative Games Although the early educational cooperative games movement faded before it could fully flower, its scholarship and record of practice remain valuable. It provides a strong foundation for contemporary educators to build upon. The current moment presents a great opportunity for a resurgence of cooperative gaming in education because kids across America—and indeed the world—have discovered them as entertainment vehicles.

Young people today are playing lots of cooperative games—online games, video games, and tabletop games. Cooperative games became culturally relevant in the mainstream beginning about 2010. I know when the trend started because, coincidentally, I had been working in the field for a year or so before it began. When I first started doing public education through my website, writing articles, and giving workshops, most people I met were unfamiliar with the term. How things have changed! Cooperative games are now a thoroughly normal play genre. The appetite for cooperative games among youth today appears synchronized with a general trend toward inclusivity, connection, and common purpose. This sensibility stands out as a hopeful sign and an opportunity for healing a bitterly divided nation.

THEORIES OF LEARNING AND PLAY SUPPORTING COOPERATIVE GAMES

The cooperative games pioneers are not the only scholars to have promoted the use of cooperative play in school. Some of our most established educational theories provide theoretical support as well. The following short summaries describe the correlation.

Froebel German educator Friedrich Froebel (1782–1852) created the first kindergarten. He was a strong and influential early advocate for play in education. He said, "Play is the highest level of child development. It is the spontaneous expression of thought and feeling . . . It . . . constitutes the source of all that can benefit the child . . . At this age, play is never trivial; it is serious and deeply significant" (Lilley, 1967, p. 84). Froebel realized that play has a holistic effect, nurturing children's social, emotional, cognitive, physical, and spiritual development (Tovey, 2020).

As history shows, Froebel's influence on American education has been tremendous. The play-filled kindergarten he invented was the norm for many years. It is only in recent decades that this standard has lost some influence in favor of "back-to-the basics" academic instruction (Zigler & Bishop-Josef, 2006).

For Froebel, play had little to do with the acquisition of declarative knowledge, and this didn't matter. The practical purpose of play in school is to nurture curiosity and a love of learning that motivate future disciplined academic study.

Froebel's choice of the term *kindergarten*, or "children's garden," reflects his belief that natural settings have unique developmental benefits. He also believed that play with geometric shapes nurtures the child. He developed toys consisting of interlocking wooden blocks that he called "gifts." These were later a source of inspiration to architect Frank Lloyd Wright (Froebel USA, 2019). Froebel was also a proponent of gentle cooperative games. Though he did not call them by this name, he created cooperative games and wrote about their ability to help children grow in important ways (Froebel, 1899). One of his games is featured in the "Play to Learn" section at the end of this chapter.

Piaget Swiss biologist and philosopher Jean Piaget (1896–1980) is credited with the now-popular notion that "play is the work" of childhood. Piaget's primary focus was on cognitive development. His ideas helped lay the foundation for *constructivism*, the theory of teaching and learning at the core of modern student-centered education. Its central idea is that knowledge must be constructed by the learner through personal experience. Knowledge cannot be poured from the teacher into the heads of passive students. Instead, learners must build knowledge through their own effort. This involves creating *schemata*, which are mental frameworks that hold ideas and beliefs in an array that appears sensible to the learner.

Play is the active, experiential process a child naturally undertakes to learn about his environment. Through play, he discovers information about the world that he uses to build, expand, and adjust his cognitive framework. If the child is deprived of play, he cannot assimilate and accommodate new information to grow knowledge frameworks.

Piaget described developmental stages of cognitive growth. Young children between ages 2 and 7 are in the *preoperational stage* of development (Wood, Smith, & Grossniklaus, 2001). At this stage, children rely particularly on pretend play, object play, and social play. They can represent objects symbolically in their minds, yet they cannot apply logic or understand cause-and-effect relations. As children enter the next stages of cognitive development beginning in the primary grades, they become more capable of using logic, reason, analysis, and other advanced cognitive capacities. Until this point, the developmentally appropriate way to stimulate cognitive development in school is through play.

Vygotsky Lev Vygotsky (1896–1934) was a Russian developmental psychologist. Like Piaget, Vygotsky studied cognitive development, but he was interested in emotional and social development as well. Vygotsky's theory is known as a *social-historical theory* of learning because it connects learning to the social and cultural context (F. Hughes, 2010; Vygotsky, 1929). Vygotsky revealed that learning and development are deeply affected by social forces. Therefore, the cultural aspects of any given educational process determine what outcomes occur. For optimal development, the teacher must provide learning experiences that utilize social forces in a strategic way.

Cooperative play and games align with Vygotsky's theory in a fundamental way because they have a strong positive effect on the classroom's social environment. This has been well documented by numerous studies that are thoroughly discussed in subsequent chapters (Goldstein, 2002; Orlick, 1981).

Vygotsky advocated several specific teaching practices that cooperative play and games relate to as well. He emphasized the importance of a particular form of cooperative play called *sociodramatic play*. In sociodramatic play, children act out adult roles collaboratively. Playing "House,"

"Doctor," and "Home Builder" are classic examples. Sociodramatic play is the most common form of social play among preschool age children (F. Hughes, 2010). Vygotsky (1930) explained that it teaches *social rules*, which are the codes of conduct that underlie forms of behavior that are deemed appropriate in any given cultural context. Learning social rules is a major component of social development. Less obviously, cooperative play in the form of sociodramatic play nurtures cognitive development, too. Social rules are abstract. Therefore, discerning how they operate is an exercise in symbolic thinking.

Vygotsky's (1930) concept of the *zone of proximal development*, or ZPD, also relates to cooperative games. The ZPD is the difference between what a child can learn on his own versus what he can learn by interacting with others, such as peers or a teacher. By working within the child's ZPD, the teacher neither overloads nor stalls the child's intellectual growth but prods it to just the right degree (F. Hughes, 2010). Cooperative games that present a challenge that students cannot meet on their own but can resolve through collaboration with their peers fits nicely within the ZPD.

Dewey John Dewey (1859–1952) was an American philosopher, educator, and leader of the progressive educational reform movement. He was probably the most popular and influential intellectual of his era, connecting progressive philosophy with education, the arts, political discourse, and psychology (Hildebrand, 2018). He advocated for women's suffrage, racial equality, and peace. As a progressive educator, Dewey renounced what he called "traditional education," that is, rote learning of information irrelevant to students' daily lives delivered via individualistic settings (Goldstein, 2002). Dewey believed that traditional education was developmentally inappropriate for children and should be replaced with experiential education—learning by doing (Williams, 2017). Further, it should involve learning in social groups (Goldstein, 2002). Dewey was an ardent supporter of play for younger children as well as an advocate of a playful attitude for people of all ages. The playful attitude is one of openness and curiosity as well as commitment and dedication. Adult work conducted with a playful attitude is meaningful to adults just as play is captivating to children, according to Dewey (Dennis, 1970).

The element of Deweyan philosophy that most specifically supports cooperative games, though, is his love of democracy. A consistent theme of his philosophical work is the idea that democracy supports human well-being better than any other form of governance. However, democracy depends on the existence of an informed and engaged citizenry that can shoulder the responsibilities of self-governance. The public schools are crucial to democracy because they are the mechanism by which each generation acquires the skills and values needed to sustain itself (Dewey, 1916). As described by Schmuck (1985), cooperation is the apex skill and value that citizens require and that schools must teach to support democracy: "Dewey argues that if humans are to live cooperatively, they must experience the living process of cooperation in the schools. Life in the classroom should represent the democratic process in microcosm, and the heart of democratic living is cooperation in groups" (p. 2).

Cooperative games teach cooperation experientially through the sharing of resources and decision-making in social groups. They are a highly effective means of teaching cooperation to everyone, even those with little or no experience of it (Cohen, 1986). How the concept of cooperative games would have delighted Dewey!

Montessori Italian physician and educator Maria Montessori (1870–1952) was a world-renowned pioneer of child-led education. She was also the innovative developer of teaching methods that have helped children of diverse abilities develop to their fullest intellectual potential. Montessori was not an advocate of imaginary play as Vygotsky was (F. Hughes, 2010). But she was certainly a proponent of using games for social, cognitive, and academic learning and development (Montessori, 1912).

Montessori's methods were gentle and kind, and this is reflected in the games she created. For example, in her Silence Game, the teacher locates herself in a corner of the room some distance from the children. Children are asked to hush. The teacher randomly calls their names in a whispering voice. When they hear their name, each child comes and sits beside the teacher until the whole group is assembled. A reading game provides another example. In this game, the teacher writes the names of different toys on cards, then puts the cards into a hat to pass around. Each child who can read picks a card. If the child can read the name of the toy written on the card, she is allowed to fetch it from a table of toys nearby. She is allowed to play with the toy as long as she wishes. Children who can read also fetch toys for those who cannot read, with the reader ceremoniously bowing to the nonreader as she presents the toy.

Cooperative games coincide with Montessori's educational priorities and methods in another very special way: Peace. Montessori was a critic of competition, which was an unusual position to take in her era. She warned that competition trains children for violence and ultimately drives a society to war. For Montessori, teaching peace was as central to the job as reading and math instruction. She said: "Averting war is the work of politicians; establishing peace is the work of educators" (Duckworth, 2006, p. 1). Accordingly, Montessori developed pedagogical methods to teach peace. These methods focused on the development of the whole child and relational skills as well as discouraging competition.

Cooperative games, of course, were conceived as a tool for peace education by Lentz and Cornelius in the 1950s, and their basic strategy is teaching cooperation and "un-teaching" the competitive attitude that children are socialized into. Montessori was right about the link between competition and war, a topic that will be discussed further in Chapter 8. In so many ways, cooperative games align with Maria Montessori's insightful views on education.

PLAYFUL LEARNING

As we have seen, the major educational theories and the associated body of research and classroom practice clearly demonstrate that play is essential in learning and child development. Yet, in today's environment, early childhood educators face strong pressure to prioritize academic skills and knowledge. Is it possible for teachers of young children to promote both play and academic learning? The approach to teaching known as *playful learning* (PL) aims to do this. The intention of PL is to combine play and learning in ways that stay true to the meaning of play yet also teach developmentally appropriate academic skills and knowledge (White, n.d.). PL is not schoolwork renamed "play"; it really is play.

PL includes both *free play* to *guided play*. "Free play" is play that children devise and lead by themselves. In "guided play" the child's activities are scaffolded by a knowledgeable adult toward a particular learning goal, though the children's actions within the play session are freely chosen by themselves. Both free play and guided play are clearly distinguishable from direct instruction, which is not a form of play at all. Rather, direct instruction is the familiar approach to teaching in which adults both initiate and tightly structure learning opportunities.

Free Play in School: Benefits and Limitations

Free play is essential for healthy child development and is especially crucial for children of kindergarten age and younger (Carlsson-Paige, 2018). However, it has both strengths and limitations when it is used for educational purposes. Its strength is that it gives children the opportunity to learn strictly through personal discovery. Learning this way is exciting, meaningful, and memorable. The limitation of free play for many teaching settings is that it is manifestly a cumbersome way to teach specific academic skills and content. For example, how could students learn the letters of the alphabet without adult guidance within the time constraints of the school calendar? Young children learn many important lessons that ultimately apply to mastering academic content through their free play. But if the teacher's goal (or requirement) is to teach academic information, guided play is generally more efficient.

Guided Play: A Playful Way to Learn Academic Subject Matter

Recall that a hallmark of play is that it is freely chosen. In keeping with this, during a guided play session, the child is free to choose what he does at any time. The teacher provides scaffolding by, for example, setting up the environment with certain kinds of toys or by asking open-ended questions, e.g., "What do you think will happen if you put that big block on the tip of your tower?" As Temple University researchers Toub, Rajan, Golinkoff, & Hirsh-Pasek wrote in 2016:

> Guided play presents an evidence-based, pedagogical sweet spot with a careful balance between constraining the learning environment and scaffolding an activity versus respecting children's agency in their play. As a child-directed activity that maintains the enjoyable nature of play within the context of an adult's developmentally appropriate, contingent, scaffolded, and goal-directed support, guided play naturally uses mechanisms that foster strong learning. (p. 134)

Cooperative games and cooperative play are at home in all playful learning settings-free play as well as guided play. In a free-play period, children are likely to initiate any number of cooperative play forms such clapping games, sociodramatic play, or working together to build a structure. There is also a practically endless variety of ways that cooperative games and play activities can be used in a guided-play format. For example, if the teacher's objective is to teach cooperative skills, he could make collaborative toys such as tea sets, a puppet theater, blocks, and puzzles available. He could prompt students to notice the benefits of cooperation or help them hone their skills with leading questions as they explore the toys. To teach academic content, a teacher could facilitate a cooperative game such as Shape It Up for math or Webbing for science. (Directions to these and other games for teaching academic content can be found in Chapter 4.) In the guided play format, the teacher invites—but does not force—children to opt in. Through sensitive prompts and open-ended questions, the teacher helps the children formalize their thoughts and observations.

MEETING CURRENT CHALLENGES IN PLAY WITH COOPERATIVE GAMES

Sadly, the kingdom of play is under siege in several respects. Can cooperative games help? Consider the following problems and solutions.

1. Premature Emphasis on Academics

The first kindergarten in America was opened in Wisconsin in 1856 (Passe, 2010). Kindergarten remained a playful affair largely aligned with Froebel's philosophy for a hundred years. In 1957, this began to change with the Soviet Union's launch of *Sputnik 1* (Dennis, 1970). The Soviet Union had won the space race, and American confidence was shaken. Policy makers heeded political pressure, discounted what was known about child development, and pushed for educational reforms intended to increase America's "global competitiveness." Play was construed as frivolous in this frame of mind.

In the ensuing decades, the educational policy pendulum has swung back and forth between whole child perspectives and the three R's model (Dennis, 1970). The No Child Left Behind (NCLB) Act of 2001 used standardized testing to enforce national curriculum standards requiring young children to demonstrate proficiency in early math and reading skills. The policy had a deep, sweeping, and lasting effect. Today, standardized tests are still used to measure the absorption of academic knowledge, despite evidence that early formal instruction can adversely affect long-term academic achievement (Katz, 2015). Teachers often feel obliged to "teach to the test," even in preschool and kindergarten. Cooperative games can help in this environment by teaching academic skills and content in a guided play format. Forget the worksheets, flash cards, and software that dress up "drill and kill" with bells and whistles. Teachers can genuinely teach through play with well-designed educational cooperative games instead.

2. Too Much Screen-Based Entertainment

Children in the United States are growing up in an information-technology and media-filled environment. Television, smartphones, and computers are integrated into the fabric of everyday life. The Internet, TV shows, videos, apps, educational software, and digital games offer stimulating diversion and an easy emotional ride at the press of a button and a few chipper clicks. But screen-based entertainment and play are not a good substitute for genuine play with real objects and people.

According to educator and developmental psychologist Diane Levin (2010), one of the problems with screens is that "Many children become dependent on the fast-paced stimulation, so the more they have the more they need" (p. 21). An even broader and deeper issue is that when authentic play is replaced with screen-based entertainment, children's ability to play and learn normally can be impaired. Teachers have noticed that classic play materials, for instance play dough, do not excite children of the digital age as they used to. Levin characterizes the overall problem as such: "The very process in which children learn is transformed in ways that undermine play, problem solving, active learning, and social development" (p. 14). Good cooperative games and noncompetitive cooperative play activities are a positive alternative to screen-based play. There is absolutely no need for technology in cooperative games.

QUESTION FOR REFLECTION

5. An electronic toy in the image of a little boy responds to input, answering questions a child asks it. Does this toy offer an experience of cooperative play?

---

3. Overall Decline in Time Spent Playing

Children are playing less these days (Carlsson-Paige, 2018). There is less time for play in school due to the pressures of standards-based learning and assessment. There is less time after school as well—due to hectic lifestyles, increased participation in after-school activities, and busy work schedules that cut down on family time. And, of course, the lure of screen-based passive entertainment reduces play time, too.

Adults can help children play more. One way is for parents to invite children to play cooperatively with them. Cooperative play and games can be made very quick for adults who have little time. Tell a riddle, cuddle a teddy bear, play a chase-and-hug game, or whatever there is time for. Teachers can address the overall decline in play by bringing as much play as possible into the classroom, for example, cooperative games that combine play with learning.

4. Violent Themes in Play

Children sometimes fight and act out violently during play. This can be the result of competition. It is common for children to experience emotional meltdowns and tantrums and want to fight when they lose competitive games. Cooperative games alleviate this problem by offering a way to play where no one can be named a loser.

A more complex example of violence in play is pretend play that features violent themes. Children engage in pretend violence in all sorts of ways, such as shooting imaginary guns and impersonating superheroes who win the day by smashing the bad guys. Pretend violence is a problem in the classroom for several reasons. It disrupts peace and orderliness; it models violence to onlookers; if it features guns, it conjures fears related to school shootings; and it often does end up in actual aggression or violence (Levin, 2003).

Children act out violence they see in the media, in their communities, or households through pretend play. This is an important way for them to process disturbing feelings. Caring adults can help children with this in appropriate settings. However, for all the reasons mentioned, violent pretend play is not appropriate at school. But how can teachers prevent it? Outright bans on violent play do not always work. One approach is to offer students the chance to draw or write. This is a means for processing violent themes and is a much better option than pretend violence (Levin, 2003). In addition, cooperative games would be a logical choice. They show that conflicts can be solved through communication and cooperation. Violence is not the only option, and it doesn't make you a hero.

5. Inequitable Access to Play for Low-Income Children

The trend toward increased academics and rigor, which has resulted in less art and music, less child choice, and less play, affects schools nationwide. However, it is more pronounced among underresourced schools in lower-income, urban communities that have a high percentage of children of color (Carlsson-Paige, 2018). Thus, the developmental disadvantages of a play-deprived education accrue disproportionately to children who suffer from the most severe economic disadvantages. Further, many of these children also lack opportunities for healthy play at home. Play deprivation for children in low-income schools is a lose-lose proposition. School-based play programs for these schools, such as Playworks, provide rays of hope. Playworks is a national nonprofit organization that places full-time coaches in low-income K–8 schools. The coaches lead organized games during recess and at other times during the day, and they provide professional development to staff. Playworks uses many cooperative games because games are selected based on their ability to create a positive school climate.

6. Decline in Nature-Based Play

As Richard Louv has told us in *Last Child in the Woods* (2008), children need relaxed time in nature to play and recreate. Tragically, modern children are not spending enough time outside in nature for a host of reasons, including perceived "stranger danger," loss of access to natural play spaces, and the availability of media and digital entertainment. The decline has given rise to "nature deficit disorder"—a common malaise with a host of mental, physical, and social symptoms. The way to solve this problem, of course, is to get children outside more often. Play, including cooperative play and games, is a great way to entice children to go outside. As camp counselors and recreation leaders know, there are legions of fun, active cooperative games to play outside.

7. The Commercialization of Play

Play is big business. Toy sales total around $30 billion each year in the United States (Toy Association, 2020). To get a slice of the pie, toy companies advertise—*to children*. The U.S. government deregulated marketing to children in 1984. For almost 40 years now, it has been legal for advertisers to market their products directly to children. Advertising works by manipulating emotions, thinking, and behavior. These changes in the child are in the interest of the advertiser, not the child.

Today, the most popular toys among children are linked to popular media characters. But much of popular media has violent themes, promotes materialistic values, or conveys gender stereotypes. In the popular media, boys are deluged with stereotypes teaching them to be physically strong and socially independent, and to use violence to solve problems. The clear message for girls is that they should be "pretty"—as defined by media images (Levin, 2010).

Can cooperative games help concerned teachers beat back these pernicious influences? Yes, in a couple of ways. Cooperative games embody the social context from which they sprang. They reflect a decidedly nonmaterialistic sensibility. Also, most cooperative games and cooperative play require no materials or just common household items. The realm of cooperative play and games is virtually commercial-free. It is true that in recent years, big companies have gotten into the act with cooperative board games and digital co-op games. Let us hope that cooperative games retain their original earnest charm and humble nature even as they become more popular. Those of us who understand the promise of cooperative games can help keep alive prosocial games that truly foster peace.

CHAPTER SUMMARY

Cooperative games are a play form in which players follow rules requiring cooperation and that stipulate that no player can be eliminated. Cooperative games, as a deliberate alternative to competitive games, were first conceived in mid-20th-century America as a tool for peace, in response to the horrors of World War II. The early cooperative games movement accomplished much, though it faded before becoming mainstream. Today there is opportunity for a revival of interest in cooperative games in education because cooperative games have become popular as an entertainment vehicle. The theoretical rationale for cooperative games aligns with the work of influential educational theorists from Froebel to Piaget to Dewey and Montessori. Cooperative games fit within the current model of play-based education known as "guided play." Play is essential to healthy child development. Unfortunately, not all children have adequate opportunity for play. Further, play itself has been under attack in many quarters of the modern world due to such factors as commercialization and diminished free time. Cooperative games can help restore healthy play in school and beyond.

Besides providing an option for healthy play, cooperative games teach the crucial skill of cooperation. The next chapter, "Learning to Cooperate," discusses this in detail.

PLAY TO LEARN—TRY THIS!

THE FROEBEL TRAVELING GAME

This game appears in *Pedagogics of the Kindergarten* by Friedrich Froebel (1899). I have edited it to make it more doable for modern readers. It is a simple game illustrated below in Figure 1.1. However, simple games such as this can have profound developmental benefits when used frequently according to Froebel's theory. In terms of contemporary social-emotional learning pedagogy, this game is a "welcoming/inclusion practice." The Collaborative for Academic, Social, and Emotional Learning (CASEL, 2019) recommends that such "signature practices" be used daily to integrate SEL throughout the school day.

Directions:

1. Children stand in a circle. The teacher says, "We will let the ball travel," and with that, the children pass a ball from one to another all the way around the circle. The teacher removes the ball from play and asks, "Which one of you would like to travel now?"
2. A child is chosen to come to the center of the circle, for example, "Lena." As Lena walks to the center, the other children sing, "Our Lena will travel now."
3. As Lena walks around the circle, she high-fives, waves, or shakes hands with each other child. Lena alternates singing with the children in the circle. She sings: "I wish you good day, good day, good day"; the other children sing, "We wish you good day, good day, good day."

Variation 1:

Rather than singing, individual children say their own name when Lena greets them. Lena in turn says, "Good morning, Juan," "Good morning, Thor," "Good morning, Arianna," and so on all the way around the circle. At the end, the children in the circle say in unison, "Good morning, Lena."

Figure 1.1. The Froebel Traveling Game gives students the chance to greet and be greeted by their peers.

Variation 2:

For older students—and for everyone when public health warrants social distancing—an elbow bump is a good alternative to a handshake (Figure 1.2). Be sure to adapt the games you use to comply with current health guidelines.

Figure 1.2. When social distancing is important, tapping elbows can be a good way to reduce physical contact.

CHAPTER 2

Learning to Cooperate

I Am Because We Are.

—African Proverb

SNOW DAY PLAY

I had been teaching values in my classes for a while, including honesty, co-operation, empathy, concentration, self-control, and courage. My method was based largely on whole-class discussions. We also read books about people who demonstrated these qualities in their lives. The students were developing a good intellectual understanding, but their behavior made it clear that something else was needed before they could integrate these values into everyday life. And then a remarkable episode occurred. One morning it snowed . . .

Snow is unusual where I live. I would have been an ogre not to go along with the children's pleas for a special recess. I stayed inside watching from the window, enjoying the unbounded exuberance of their play. In the space of a few minutes, however, the scene shifted dramatically. First, it was an inadvertent shove that landed someone on the ground, then a wayward snowball hitting another child in the face. Within minutes the whole class seemed angry with one another. I rang the bell and called the students in.

After a calming-down period, I asked everyone to join me in the middle of the carpet for a discussion circle. "Can we go outside again?" someone asked. "Only on one condition," I responded, reminding everyone of the topic of cooperation we had been discussing. They eagerly agreed to cooperate. When they returned to the playground, at first there were a few nervous glances, but gradually everyone settled in to wholesome, *cooperative* play, including games and playful projects they made up on their own.

About a half-hour later, I signaled for recess to end. We re-formed our discussion circle, and I asked which recess they had enjoyed more. Every hand quickly went up in favor of the second one. Everyone agreed that the practice of cooperation had made all the difference. If I had any doubts

---

about the power of this incident, they evaporated as I watched the children maintain their cooperation over the following weeks and months.

Here was the alternative I had been searching for to take values instruction beyond the realm of indoctrination. My students had discovered how the quality of cooperation could make their recesses more enjoyable. The direct, personal experience of cooperation through play made all the difference.

—Adapted from Michael Nitai Deranja (2004)

Cooperative games are equal parts play and cooperation. Playing a cooperative game is an experience of play. Equally, it is an experience of cooperation. Play is beneficial for young people and old people—and even for nonhuman animals—in myriad ways. And so is cooperation! It only makes sense that the marriage of two such fine faculties—play and cooperation—would be rich in benefits, too.

In the previous chapter, we examined the nature of play, looked at the reasons why it belongs in school, and discussed the ways in which cooperative games manifest the power of play. In this chapter, we do the same for cooperation. It's time for Round 2 in our exploration of the building blocks of cooperative games.

UNDERSTANDING COOPERATION

Cooperation is to community as oxygen is to breathing. It is the essential and ever-present element that fuels the flow of life. Reflect on the cooperation needed to raise a family, have a party, run a school, build a bridge, or fight a wildfire. Without cooperation, human society would be impossible.

Psychologists define cooperation this way: Cooperation is "a process whereby two or more individuals work together toward the attainment of a mutual goal or complementary goals" (American Psychological Association, 2020). Thus, cooperation has two components: a common goal (or goals) and an organized effort to achieve the shared goal(s).

Cooperation is thus quite simple in its essence. But it has far-reaching effects in human affairs because it accomplishes two things that are of the most fundamental importance:

- Cooperation makes work easier.
- Cooperation creates social bonds.

Stop for a moment to appreciate how integral these effects of cooperation are to peace, happiness, and prosperity.

FORMS OF COOPERATION

Consider the following forms of cooperation. Notice how they each aid productivity and/or help us get along together.

Multiplication of Effort

Cooperation sometimes involves everyone in a group doing the same task so all can benefit from the multiplication of effort. This happens when neighbors pitch in to weed a community garden or friends bring their favorite dishes to a potluck party. "Many hands make light work," as the saying goes.

Division of Labor

Cooperation can also consist of individuals performing different tasks toward the group's shared goal. For example, workers in a school district—teachers, administrators, janitors, groundskeepers—pool their skills to provide a positive educational experience for students. This kind of cooperation involves a division of labor. It taps diverse skills and talents. It enhances creative efforts, complex problem-solving, and efficiency, too. "Two heads are better than one," as they say.

Pragmatism and Compromise

Groups that have little in common can cooperate to achieve specific goals amidst divergent overall agendas. This kind of cooperation can be temporary and fragile. It requires groups to bend to accommodate differing perspectives. It is achieved through a pragmatic focus on shared interests rather than differences that could be divisive. For example, nations must engage in this sort of cooperation to forge climate change agreements or sign treaties to end a war. Political coalitions are also built from pragmatic intergroup cooperation.

Friendly Cooperation

Psychologists have identified another type of cooperation: *friendly cooperation* (Ogburn & Nimkoff, 1958). Humans are social animals. We need one another's company for our own happiness and psychological well-being. We feel lonely on our own. Indeed, people languish and can even die from social isolation. Conversely, we have a great capacity for making one another happy and healthy just by mutual listening, playing together, and supporting one another emotionally. Friendly cooperation serves an emotional and psychological goal rather than a material one. Dances, social clubs, dates, caring phone chats, and birthday parties are examples of friendly cooperation.

Helping Cooperation

Individuals may also take part in *helping cooperation*. In helping cooperation, members of a group join forces to assist people in need who are not members of the group (Ogburn & Nimkoff, 1958). A search and rescue team exemplifies helping cooperation. A holiday toy drive is another example. Charity organizations of all kinds operate on the basis of helping cooperation. So do nations, when citizens join together to provide a social safety net that protects the poor, disabled, elderly, or other vulnerable populations.

WHAT COOPERATION IS NOT

Cooperation Does Not Equal Obedience

Note that there's a behavior sometimes labeled "cooperation" that doesn't fit the pattern. In everyday language, the term *cooperation* can describe obedience or compliance with an authority figure. For example, a disciplinarian may intone: "Cooperate with me, little boy, or you will be punished!" In a totalitarian regime, citizens may be forced to "cooperate" with authorities by overlooking corruption or yielding to oppressive practices. But these are examples of *obedience* in the face of coercion. True cooperation is not obedience to authority. It involves parties working toward a mutually desired goal, rather than the passive submission of persons stripped of their autonomy.

Cooperation Is Not Really Teamwork

Another thing cooperation isn't is "teamwork." *Teamwork* can refer to cooperative activities, but it can also mean *intergroup competition*—which is competition between groups. When teamwork amounts to intergroup competition, it carries the social and psychological risks that are associated with all of the forms of competition. This is discussed more fully in Chapter 3.

Cooperation Is Not a Moral Precept

If you are getting the impression that cooperation is a universally positive social phenomenon, a little reflection shows this is not the case. Cooperation is not a moral precept. It is not always a force for good. Students cooperate by sharing answers to cheat on an exam. Gang members cooperate to sell drugs on a street corner. Bullies cooperate to victimize a peer. Any coordinated effort by people toward a shared objective constitutes cooperation.

For all the good that is accomplished through human cooperation, people cooperate to do harmful things, too.

What distinguishes prosocial cooperation from the destructive version? Two factors seem important: the nature of the goal and the degree of inclusivity. Is the goal of a given cooperative effort a prosocial one—is the intention to help others? And how inclusive is the distribution of benefits? A cooperative effort that seeks to benefit all serves the "common good." This is cooperation in its maximally prosocial and ideal sense, as is practiced in cooperative games.

QUESTIONS FOR REFLECTION

1. What kinds of cooperation have you participated in today? Describe them.
2. Recall a time when you experienced a sense of harmony in a social group. Was cooperation involved? Describe.
3. A coach says that schoolchildren learn cooperation through after-school sports. In what sense is this true? In what sense is it not true?

ROOTS OF COOPERATION

As we know, cooperation is vital. And yet, as we look around, we see it so often lacking. In the family, at work and school, and in the political process, people conspicuously fail to cooperate on a regular basis. Humanity seems to be trapped in a paradox. We require cooperation to survive and thrive, but we appear incapable of sustaining it.

Cooperation and the Brain

However, hope lies in the fact that the motivation to cooperate is part of our basic nature. It is deeply rooted in the human psyche—and in the brain. Evidence comes from the field of neuroscience. In recent years, neuroscientists have begun to examine the neural activity associated with cooperative behavior. There is a small structure within the brain called the *ventral striatum*. It is part of the brain's reward system. When a person engages in something pleasurable, such as tasting a juicy strawberry or watching a beautiful sunset, their ventral striatum becomes more active. In laboratory experiments, neuroscientists have used brain-imaging technology to observe that when test subjects cooperate, their brains become excited in this way (Stallen, Griffioen, & Sanfey, 2017). Cooperation, literally, feels good.

Cooperation and Evolutionary Biology

Cooperation appears to be encoded in our genes. And why wouldn't it be? Cooperation is endemic across the spectrum of life. Bees cooperate to make honey; cells regulate their own division to avoid causing cancer; lionesses suckle one another's offspring; and whales and dolphins play together. In our culture, we have attributed exaggerated importance to competition. As Martin Nowak (2012), professor of biology and mathematics at Harvard, says, "My work indicates that instead of opposing competition, cooperation has operated alongside it from the get-go to shape the evolution of life on earth, from the first cells to *homo sapiens*" (p. 36). Further to this point: Did you know that the phrase "survival of the fittest" was coined not by Charles Darwin, but by industrialist Herbert Spencer? (Kohn, 1986). Evolutionary biologist Stephen J. Gould said, "The equation of competition with success is merely a cultural prejudice. . . . Success defined as leaving more offspring can . . . be attained by a large variety of strategies—including mutualism and symbiosis—that we would call cooperative" (Kohn, 1986, p 21.)

Of all species, homo sapiens are the most outstanding cooperators of all. Our complex societies—built upon the division of labor, nuanced cultural norms, intricate social institutions, complex technologies, and development of languages, mathematics, and science—are not the products of individual effort but are the fruits of cooperation. According to anthropologist Curtis Marean (2015), our "genetically encoded penchant for cooperation," combined with our distinctive intelligence, is what enabled homo sapiens to inhabit all of Earth's continents, something no other species has managed to do (p. 34).

In *Why We Cooperate,* evolutionary anthropologist Michael Tomasello (2009) explains why his studies show that the drive to cooperate is inborn—indelible—rather than learned. He puts it the following way:

> One of the great debates in Western Civilization is whether humans are born cooperative and helpful and society later corrupts them (e.g. Rousseau), or whether they are born selfish and unhelpful and society teaches them better (e.g. Hobbes). As with all great debates, both arguments undoubtedly have some truth on their side. Here I defend a thesis that mainly sides with Rousseau's take on things but adds some critical complexities. . . . I will argue and present evidence that from around their first birthdays . . . human children are already cooperative and helpful in many, though obviously not all, situations. And they do not learn it from adults; it comes naturally. . . . But later . . . children's relatively indiscriminate cooperativeness becomes mediated by such influences as their judgment of likely reciprocity and their concern for how others in the group might judge them . . . And they begin to internalize many culturally specific norms for how we do things. (pp. 3–4)

Thus, perhaps *both* the drive to cooperate and its fragility are innately human. It is our nature to cooperate, but under the influence of various pressures, we pursue selfish interests. An urgent question that researchers and public policy makers are now exploring is: How can cooperation be supported in public life? Educators have part of the answer: *Teach it.*

QUESTIONS FOR REFLECTION

4. Neuroscience, evolutionary biology, and anthropology suggest that the drive to cooperate is an inherent trait of human beings. However, this drive may only be activated within social groups. Is this a problem for peace? Discuss.
5. How do cooperative games provide practice in universal cooperation, i.e., cooperation beyond the members of one's own social group?

SOCIAL INTERDEPENDENCE THEORY: COOPERATION VERSUS COMPETITION

A Postwar Social-Psychological Theory

The social effects of cooperation and competition have been studied extensively over the past 80 years. *Social interdependence theory*, developed by social psychologist Morton Deutsch of Columbia University, is the centerpiece of this body of work. Deutsch developed the theory in the late 1940s, shortly after serving in the Air Force during World War II. He described his motivation: "I was concerned with issues of war and peace and whether the members of the recently formed UN Security Council would be cooperative or competitive. These were my concerns and I formulated my theory and conducted my research" (Johnson & Johnson, 2011, p. 60).

Deutsch's concerns launched a fabulously fruitful investigation. His research findings have been validated by hundreds of subsequent researchers and a vast canon of empirical studies (Coleman, 2017). Accordingly, his work has had a profound impact across the social sciences.

Social interdependence theory shows that whether people cooperate or compete to achieve their goals determines numerous social processes and that these social effects in turn determine the extent to which goals are achieved. When people cooperate, they perceive that they can succeed only if those with whom they are linked also succeed in attaining their goals. This is called *positive interdependence*. When people compete, on the other hand, individuals perceive that they can obtain their goals only to the extent that those with whom they are linked fail to achieve theirs (Johnson & Johnson, 2011). This is called *negative interdependence.*

Positive interdependence induces *promotive interaction*, behavior such as helping and encouraging. Negative interdependence produces *oppositional interaction*, behavior such as discouraging and obstructing each other's efforts. The social and emotional concomitants of promotive and oppositional interaction, unsurprisingly, are diametrically opposed. Cooperation is associated with mutual liking, friendliness, trust, and various prosocial inclinations. Competition tends to induce "tactics of coercion and threat, enhancement of power differences, deceptive communication, and striving to 'win' in conflicts" (Johnson & Johnson, 2011, p. 42).

The theory of social interdependence, and the empirical evidence supporting it, also show that the social effects of cooperation and competition impact goal achievement. Not surprisingly, the theory shows that the prosocial behavior and mutual support and coordination associated with cooperation result in better goal attainment than the social effects of competition (Deutsch, 1949b). After all, everyday observation can show the link between cooperation and productivity as well. As a thought experiment, close your eyes and recall a time when you were in a group that achieved a goal everyone cared about. Was there an overall tone of cooperation or competition among group members?

The Crude Law of Social Relations

Deutsch's *crude law of social relations* demonstrates that both cooperation and competition are self-reinforcing. The processes and social effects that cooperation elicits (for example, helping another person) tend to elicit more cooperation. Likewise, the processes and effects of competition tend to beget more competition. If you and I are getting along cooperatively but then I sabotage you, you will probably respond noncooperatively to me. Once cooperation is violated, it no longer self-propagates.

All in all, social interdependence theory and the mountain of empirical evidence supporting it establish that competition is correlated to social discord at levels up to and including outright aggression, diminished outcomes, and psychological stress. Cooperation leads to more peaceful and positive relationships, better achievement, and greater psychological health (Deutsch, 1949a; Johnson & Johnson, 2008).

Value of Relationship Variables to Study Behavior

Social interdependence theory focuses on relationship variables rather than individual variables. This is a novel frame of investigation. Most psychological theories locate the causes of individual behavior inside the individual.

They investigate individual variables such as personality traits, values, skills, aptitudes, brain chemistry, and genes. The theory of social interdependence, however, focuses on relationship variables, that is, variables that reside between or among parties.

It is true that cooperativeness and competitiveness can be productively viewed in terms of individual variables. Interesting correlations exist between individual variables such as personality traits and cooperative or competitive behavior (Garcia, Tor, & Schiff, 2013). However, social interdependence theory shows that relationship dynamics—how people interact with and treat each other—are very highly determinative of whether cooperation or competition is expressed (Johnson & Johnson, 2011). There is a tendency to ascribe behavior to individual variables, in research and in our own ways of making sense of the world. It is a more concrete way of looking at things and therefore easier to understand. However, it is more appropriate and strategic for teachers to focus on relationship variables when it comes to understanding and nurturing cooperative behavior. Teachers cannot influence personality traits or aptitudes—nor brain chemistry nor genes! It is not within the bounds of their position to attempt to do so. But it is well within the power and the scope of teachers to teach cooperation by teaching their students positive relationship skills.

LEARNING COOPERATION IN SCHOOL

Why teach cooperation in school? A couple of practical reasons are immediately clear:

- Effective classroom management depends on cooperation.
- Cooperative skills enhance academic achievement.

First, if students do not cooperate with the teacher and one another, there is chaos and confusion in the class. Teaching cooperative skills and norms is part and parcel of positive discipline and other good classroom-management strategies. And second, cooperation enhances academic achievement. Students who learn to cooperate can form study groups, help each other with assignments, and encourage each other to do their best. Students need to be able to cooperate to succeed in *cooperative learning settings*. According to a meta-analysis of 122 related studies, cooperative learning supports academic achievement and higher-order thinking better than competitive or individualistic arrangements (Johnson, Johnson, Murayama, & Nelson, 1981). Students who do not cooperate well miss out on the benefits of cooperative learning, and they bring down others who depend upon them as well.

In the big picture, beyond the four walls of the classroom, cooperation is so fundamentally critical for success in personal relationships and for peaceful and productive group behavior that it is hard to imagine any more worthy subject to teach. And let us not forget that the aggregate result of teaching cooperation in the schools, according to John Dewey (1916), is nothing less than the survival of a thriving democracy. Surely cooperation is a subject worth teaching, re-teaching, and teaching again. We all need to know how to work together and be reminded again and again why this is important. As stated at the beginning of this chapter, society without coop-eration is impossible.

TEACHING COOPERATION THROUGH PLAY AND GAMES

Cooperation is sometimes taught as an academic topic and sometimes as a practical skill. When presented as a topic, students learn about the social phenomenon of cooperation. When taught as a skill, they learn how to do it themselves. Research shows that if the ultimate goal is teaching cooperative behavior, it is best to teach cooperation both ways: as a social phenomenon and as a set of cooperative subskills such as helping, sharing, negotiating, and so on (Cohen, 1986).

Teaching the Topic of Cooperation

How can the topic of cooperation be taught? Younger children might lis-ten to stories, sing songs, and look at pictures of people or animals work-ing and playing together to understand the nature of cooperation. Older kids can read stories, biographies, and case studies highlighting the advantages of collaboration. They can study the various types of cooperation. College stu-dents can explore the topic in wide-ranging courses such as social psychology, evolutionary biology, anthropology, mathematics, political science, peace and conflict studies, business, economics, and education.

Note that many cooperative board games teach cooperation both ways—as a topic and a skill set. For example, in Pandemic, Max, or Save the Whales, the game narrative showcases cooperation as a force for good in the real world. Meanwhile, the game mechanics teach cooperative skills by requir-ing players to pool resources and decision-making.

Teaching Cooperative Skills

When it comes to teaching cooperative skills, there are two basic methods to choose from: cooperative learning (also called *group work*) and cooperative games. These are much alike. They both strive to replace the negative social effects of competition with the positive effects of cooperation. They can both be effective (Goldstein, 2002). But they have different strengths and limita-tions. When and why would you choose cooperative games?

Cooperative games, of course, involve play. By definition, play is enjoyable, engaging, and voluntary, and it is free of extrinsic goals and judgments as well (Toub et al., 2016). So when students engage in cooperative play, they are absorbed in fun. They are not worried about anything in the real world. They may even be able to suspend their social identities and relate to one another without any sense of separation as they engage in the fluid and magical world of play.

On the other hand, cooperative learning tasks involve work. The tasks are often made intentionally complex so that they show how cooperation can make difficult work easier, improve the quality of a product, and foster constructive social interchange (Cohen, 1986). Cooperative learning tasks can be fun, too, but that is not their primary focus.

In preschool and the younger grades, play is developmentally appropriate and complex academic work tasks are not (Singer, Michnick Golinkoff, & Hirsh-Pasek, 2006). Thus, cooperative games are an easy choice for teachers of young children.

In the older grades, cooperative learning can be a fine choice. If the intention is to teach academic subjects and cooperation at the same time, cooperative learning makes sense. Hundreds of studies have shown that it imparts social skills while developing academic skills and knowledge (Johnson & Johnson, 1991). Note that it is indeed possible to use cooperative games to teach academic content plus cooperation, too. However, cooperative learning is a much more established and refined method for this. Its great success in classrooms all around the world, going all the way back to the 1970s, assures that cooperative learning will remain the primary option for teaching academic content and social skills together. (See Chapter 6 for further discussion of cooperative learning.)

However, if the goal is simply teaching cooperative behavior, cooperative games may be a better option. They have several practical advantages. A big advantage is that cooperative games are easy and quick to implement. They are inexpensive, uncomplicated, and require no prior skills or knowledge. Whereas experts advise that cooperative learning should be preceded by cooperative training, there are many cooperative games that just about everyone can do on a moment's notice. Indeed, experts recommend cooperative games as the very training for cooperative learning (Cohen, 1986).

Another advantage is their inclusivity. The best cooperative games for whole-class learning are fun and simple. This assures that students of varying abilities can interact with one another at the same time.

The fun factor is also a great advantage. Affect is key to learning, after all. When students enjoy a game, they are intrinsically motivated to keep playing it, practicing their developing cooperative skills all the while.

WHAT RESEARCH SAYS ABOUT TEACHING
COOPERATION THROUGH GAMES

Terry Orlick, whom I introduced in the Introduction as a pioneer of cooperative games, produced some of earliest studies showing that cooperative games teach cooperative skills. For example, Orlick conducted a study in 1978 with colleagues McNally and O'Hara that they summarized this way:

> The cooperative games concept has been developed to increase cooperation among people in and out of game situations. This article discusses how cooperative behavior has been increased in children through a cooperative games program. The study conducted observed 87 kindergartners divided into traditional games and cooperative games groups. Prior to the study, these two groups displayed similar levels of cooperative behavior. As the games program progressed the children in the cooperative games groups showed an increase in cooperative behaviors. This cooperative behavior was observed over time to be displayed in other activities than the game situations. (p. 203)

Another early researcher of cooperative games was Arnold P. Goldstein of Syracuse University. Goldstein was an international authority on aggression as well as a professor of education and psychology. He developed a cooperation training program for at-risk youth using cooperative games, researched cooperative games, and conducted meta-analyses on this subject. Goldstein (2002) wrote:

> Cooperative play indeed enhances cooperation and a number of its prosocial concomitants. Bryant and Crockenberg (1974) and Jacovino (1980) have each demonstrated the potency of cooperative games for enhancing such components of cooperation as mutual concern, attentiveness to feelings of obligation for other students, and mutual liking. DeVries, Muse, and Wells (1971), have successfully used cooperative games to produce a peer climate combining academic involvement and peer encouragement. In a study by DeVries, Edwards, and Wells (1974), cooperative games increased divergent thinking, time on task, student preference for cooperative versus competitive activities, and student belief that peers had a substantial interest in one's academic success. Cook (1969), and DeVries & Edwards (1973) also successfully employed cooperative games to increase cooperative behavior between interracial groups . . . In all, cooperative gaming, much like cooperative learning, has been shown to yield reliable and substantial cooperation-enhancing and related prosocial effects. (p. 148)

Elizabeth G. Cohen, scholar of cooperative learning, used cooperative games to create a cooperative training program. On the basis of her research while at Stanford University, Cohen concluded that cooperative games can teach the cooperative skills and attitudes needed for more complex cooperation involved in cooperative learning tasks. In *Designing Groupwork: Strategies for the Heterogeneous Classroom* (1986), she wrote: "Preparing students for cooperative groups requires you to decide which [cooperative] norms and skills will be needed for the groupwork you have in mind. These norms are best taught through exercises and games" (p. 36).

Finally, consider the study "Cooperative Games: A Way to Modify Aggressive and Cooperative Behaviors in Young Children" by April Bay-Hinitz, Robert F. Peterson, and H. Robert Quilitch of the University of Nevada, Reno (1994). The authors investigated the effects of competitive and cooperative games on both cooperative as well as aggressive behavior of children ages 4 and 5. This study was groundbreaking because it investigated not only prosocial behavior but also aggression. (Aggression will be discussed in more detail in Chapter 8.) The researchers reported unambiguous findings: *Cooperative behavior increased and aggression decreased during cooperative games; conversely, competitive games were followed by increases in competitive behavior and aggression and decreases in cooperative behavior.* Importantly, the behavior associated with cooperative games generalized to free play and other social interactions after the games.

The researchers defined cooperative behavior as "a behavior that was directed toward another child and that involved a shared, reciprocal, mutual, or helpful quality." Under that definition, these are the particular behaviors correlated with cooperative games:

> Cooperative behavior included: (a) sharing, assisting, or executing a task with another child, working toward a common goal, sharing material, or explicitly helping another child; (b) physically supporting another child (for example one child carrying another child or helping another child off the ground or over a barrier), or engaging in physical contact of an affectionate nature (for example linking arms, holding hands, embracing, kissing, or patting a child on the back); or (c) verbal behavior such as giving a child instruction on how to do something, verbally offering to help or to share, or agreeing to a request made by another child. (pp. 437–438)

Cooperative behavior in all its glory—a valuable prize we win by playing together.

CHAPTER SUMMARY

Cooperative games teach cooperation, and cooperation is one of the most important things that students can learn in school. Humans have a basic drive to cooperate that is brain-based and rooted in evolutionary biology. It makes work easier and forges social bonds. This gives cooperation virtually infinite practical applicability. Social interdependence theory shows that the social effects of cooperation and competition are inverse. In a nutshell, cooperation promotes harmony and productivity, while competition fosters conflict and negative social effects from envy to aggression.

The two hands-on approaches to teaching cooperative skills are cooperative learning (or group work) and cooperative games. Cooperative games have certain advantages because they are a form of play. Research validates what we would predict: well-designed cooperative games teach cooperative social skills and motivation, increasing cooperative behavior. Besides teaching cooperation, cooperative games are an antidote to excessive, unexamined competition. Why is this important? Read on to Chapter 3, "Rethinking Competition"!

PLAY TO LEARN—TRY THIS!

COOPERATIVE TIC-TAC-TOE

Ruth Cornelius and Theo Lentz (1950), co-authors of the first discourse on cooperative games, invented Cooperative Tic-Tac-Toe. They summed up the rationale for using cooperative games to teach cooperation in school this way:

- Cooperative attitudes are desirable.
- Cooperative attitudes can be learned.
- Play is a means for acquiring attitudes.
- Cooperative games help to develop cooperative attitudes. (p. 16)

Directions:

Draw a hash-mark figure as you would for traditional *tic-tac-toe,* as shown in Figure 2.1 The first player writes a number in one space, the next player writes the next number, and the third player writes a third number so that all three numbers are in a single row or column. When the row or column is complete, add up the numbers. This sum is the number to strive for in all succeeding plays. In subsequent turns, the players write a number in a space, attempting to have all rows and columns add up to the first sum. Numbers must be less than 10, and no number (except the first three that were added to make the initial row or column) can be repeated. A challenge, but possible!

Variation:

To make this game easier, allow numbers to be repeated as often as players like.

Figure 2.1. Cooperative Tic-Tac-Toe is a puzzle that helps students build math and cognitive skills while strengthening communication and camaraderie.

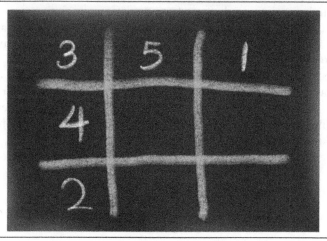

CHAPTER 3

Rethinking Competition

Everyone talks about peace, but no one educates for peace. In this world,
they educate for competition, and competition is the beginning of war.

—Maria Montessori

Parents await the results breathlessly in folding chairs while children
fidget on the gymnasium floor. This is the end-of-year awards ceremony
at A-1 Elementary School. Introductory remarks have been made and
niceties exchanged. Now it is time for the main event, the beef, that part
of the show that gets the blood pumping. Who among the children will
receive awards and who won't? Who will wear the Best Citizen medal?
Who will win the blue-ribbon fitness award? Even more to the point: Who
will win the highest prize in this mini-kingdom—the exalted Principal's
Award?

One student from each grade level receives the Principal's Award
each year. Though it is the top honor, it is not the final competition. Everyone knows that a few kids win the prize multiple years. These anointed
ones are truly the Best of the Best. On the other end of the spectrum are
the children who never win any awards. They sit ingloriously year after
year on the linoleum floor watching other kids receive all the praise.

Author's observation of neighborhood school, 2005

QUESTION FOR REFLECTION

1. How might a highly competitive school culture such as we see at
A-1 Elementary shape the behavior of students over time? How
might educational outcomes differ for "winners" versus "losers"?

As we have seen in Chapters 1 and 2, cooperative games combine two
healthy modes of behavior that help people learn, get along together, and
enjoy themselves: play and cooperation. And so there is a highly positive

argument for teaching with games based on fun collaboration. Indeed, teachers are attracted to cooperative games for all their benefits.

But there is another, more cautionary rationale for using cooperative games in education: they prompt us to rethink competition. Competition is often lauded, but it is generally unexamined and poorly understood. It is vital for educators to understand the potential harm associated with competition and utilize appropriate counter measures.

DEFINING TERMS

Competition is one of the three ways that people pursue their goals. The other two are cooperation and individualism. To keep our conversation about competition clear, we need a precise understanding of each of these terms. They are defined as follows:

- *Competition* is a social arrangement in which two or more parties attempt to achieve a goal that cannot be fulfilled by everyone. In other words, it is a condition of "mutually exclusive goal attainment" (Kohn, 1986, p. 4).
- *Cooperation* is "a process whereby two or more individuals work together toward the attainment of a mutual goal or complementary goals" (American Psychological Association, 2020).
- *Individualism* is a mode by which an individual pursues a goal, neither competing nor cooperating with anyone else. It is the "solitary striving for goals apart from all other humans" (Johnson & Johnson, 1991, p. 14).

Note that both competition and cooperation are forms of social interaction. This means that there is really no such thing as competing against oneself. When we "compete against ourselves," we are actually striving to do our "personal best." That is, we measure our progress against our own performance markers. This is an individualistic effort. Competition, on the other hand, requires that two or more parties participate.

In everyday life, we rarely see examples of pure competition. Actual, unadulterated competition is strictly zero-sum: I win because you lose. The results of this starkly adversarial arrangement are potentially so damaging that we usually put social rules in place to soften the blows. Some of these social rules mitigate the "agony of defeat." That is, they reduce the psychological pain, interpersonal stress, or material impact of losing. For example, winners and losers might shake hands after a sports competition and say, "It's only a game." Winners are often advised to avoid boasting, and losers are expected to refrain from angry outbursts. These conventions of sportsmanship help reduce social-psychological impacts of competition and preserve relationships. The material impact of losing may be mitigated with other conventions. For example, consolation prizes or 2nd- and 3rd-place prizes may be offered.

We also use social rules that relate to fairness to make competition work. Fairness rules aim to create a "level playing field" and assure a "fair fight" so that all participants have the chance to win. For example, a 1st-grade student would not normally be pitted against a 5th-grader in a math contest.

These measures alone do not make competition sustainable. Left un-regulated, competition tends to extinguish itself because winning begets more winning. It works like this: The winner of the first round of a contest gains assets that help to win in the next round (money, brand recognition, confidence, etc.). With each round, advantage accumulates. Eventually, the initial winner acquires so much advantage that she becomes impossible to beat. At this stage, disadvantaged players have no ability or incentive to compete. The contest collapses. Social rules are needed to prop up the competition and keep it going. Antitrust laws are an example. As the Federal Trade Commission puts it: "The antitrust laws prohibit conduct of a single firm that unreasonably restrains competition by creating or maintaining monopoly power" (Federal Trade Commission, 2020).

Competition is not just mitigated by social rules to reduce its harm or to keep it going. In practice, competition often occurs commingled with a significant measure of cooperation. In the case of business, the word "coopetition" describes collaborative ventures among competitors. Even professional sports, which are so emblematic of competition, can involve cooperation between opposing teams. However, the ratio of competition to cooperation varies along a spectrum. "Cutthroat competitions" are concentrated examples that approximate pure competition, while "friendly competitions" are more diluted contests that feature a greater degree of cooperation or lean heavily on social rules that soften negative impacts.

If competition is often mitigated by cooperative measures that reduce potential harm, what's the problem? Unfortunately, the social rules buffering it often fail. Depending on the situational and personality variables in a given instance, the pressure to win may overwhelm the social contract or cooperative behaviors that keep it safe. Then the drive to conquer is unleashed in full force, and the stage is set for a variety of damaging effects.

QUESTION FOR REFLECTION

2. In what ways is competition a positive factor in everyday life? Write down your answer, read the following section, then answer the question again. Has your opinion changed?

DOCUMENTED DOWNSIDES OF COMPETITION

What do we know, specifically, about the negative consequences of competition? Consider the following list of observed effects. It is gathered from a large body of research and scholarship on the subject.

Competition Interferes With Higher-Order Thinking

If the question is, "Do students perform better on academic tasks when they compete against each other?," the answer is, "No." There are hundreds of studies that prove the point. For example, as pointed out in Chapter 2, a meta-analysis conducted at the University of Minnesota examined 122 studies comparing educational achievement in competitive, cooperative, and individualistic settings. The results? Cooperatively structured tasks promoted higher achievement than competitively structured tasks in 65 studies, 8 studies favored competition, and 36 studies found no statistical difference. In the rare cases that competition benefited performance, the evaluated tasks were simple or rote, rather than complex or creative (Johnson et al., 1981). If the goal is to promote higher-order thinking, creativity, and deep engagement with academic content, the data say that competition is not the way.

Competition Inhibits Complex Problem-Solving

Since competition inhibits the free exchange of ideas and sharing of resources, complex problems are harder to solve in highly competitive milieus. Charles Zastrow (2009), who studies social welfare, attests to this:

> The negative consequences of competition in problem-solving are numerous. Competition decreases creativity, coordination of effort, division of labor, helping and sharing, and cohesion. Competition promotes ineffective communication, suspicion and mistrust, high anxiety about goal accomplishment, negative self-attitudes, animosity between group members, and negative attitudes toward the group and its tasks. Competition also encourages the rejection of differences of opinion, divergent thinking, and cultural and individual differences. A competitive atmosphere leads to a low effectiveness in solving complex problems. (p. 79)

Competition Decreases Intrinsic Motivation

Competition provides *extrinsic* rewards—rewards outside the task itself—like status, grades, blue ribbons, money, and so on. In the long run, studies reveal a counterintuitive finding: extrinsic rewards actually *decrease* personal motivation (Kohn, 1986). Extrinsic rewards are flashy compared with the intrinsic rewards of doing an enjoyable or helpful task. When we are rewarded in competition, we become driven like mice in a maze lusting for that big piece of cheese. Our inner compass cannot direct us to what we really want when our attention is riveted on external rewards.

An experiment done by motivational psychologist Edward Deci and his colleagues shows this effect. Two groups of college students were asked to solve a puzzle. Those in one group competed while those in the other group did not. Upon finishing their task, the students were given the opportunity to play with a new puzzle. Students from the competitive group were less motivated compared to students from the noncompetitive group, who wanted to keep playing. Deci, Betley, Kahle, Abrams, and Porac summarized their study in 1981: "It appears that when people are instructed to compete in an activity, they begin to see that activity as an instrument for winning rather than as an activity which is . . . rewarding in its own right" (p. 82).

Competition Increases Ego-Oriented Motivation

Students' *motivational beliefs* are their opinions, judgments, and values regarding, for example, a school subject. Motivational beliefs underlie thinking, feeling, and action. They develop in response to prior learning experiences, the teacher-student relationship, social comparisons, and more. Motivational beliefs are a strong indicator of both engagement and performance. That is because students who have favorable motivational beliefs utilize more effective learning strategies.

Sometimes students undertake learning tasks because they want to learn a skill or investigate a subject. This is called a "mastery-oriented" motivation. On the other hand, they may be more concerned about how their performance looks in the eyes of others—whether it raises or lowers their social status. This is called "ego orientation." Mastery orientation reflects favorable motivational beliefs and correlates with higher engagement and performance (Boekaerts, 2002).

Competitive classrooms breed ego-oriented motivational beliefs. According to the International Bureau of Education in a research report: "Teachers who highlight evaluation procedures, give public feedback, frequently make social comparisons and refer to individual abilities create a competitive atmosphere and elicit ego-oriented thoughts and feelings" (Boekaerts, 2002, p. 15).

Competition Arouses Anxiety

By definition, contests create losers. In a society where the label "loser" is deeply stigmatizing, it is reasonable to feel anxious about being identified this way. Besides the stigma of losing, competitive encounters also arouse anxiety because they involve risk and uncertainty. There is no assurance of winning in any contest, and it is common for there to be many more losers than winners. The threat of losing evokes anxiety because it represents the possibility of disappointment and deprivation. Winning can cause anxiety, too. Winners may justifiably suspect that their peers will feel jealous and resentful. And if one's identity depends on being a "winner," the prospect of losing threatens identity and feelings of self-worth (Kohn, 1986).

Anxiety that arises from competition can be chronic, with debilitating long-term effects. A 2015 study examined the relationship between perceived competition and anxiety in 40,350 college students from 70 institutions. The results were clear: "Students who perceive their classroom environments to be very competitive have 37% higher odds of screening positive for depression and 69% higher odds of screening positive for anxiety" (Posselt & Lipson, 2016, p. 980). To the extent that anxiety makes school frightening and unpleasant, it inhibits academic achievement. Students who screen positive for anxiety have lower grades and are at higher risk for dropping out of school. This suggests that insofar as competition contributes to anxiety in school, it undermines academic success.

Psychoanalyst Rollo May put all of this bluntly. He concluded, upon completing his pioneering study *Anxiety in America,* that "competition is the most pervasive occasion for anxiety in our culture" (May, 1977 p. 173).

Competition Shifts Focus From Process to Product

When teachers introduce the competitive element to a learning situation, it adds a sense of external urgency and drama. Participants accordingly shift their attention from the task itself to the effects of winning or losing a contest. Thinking moves from reasoning, learning, creating, or investigating academic subject matter to strategizing about how to produce a winning product. This is a shift of attention from process to product (Shindler, 2017).

Competition Relates to Lowered Self-Esteem

Is a competitive attitude an indicator of high self-esteem? Research says, "No." A study by University of Minnesota psychologists probed the relationship between self-esteem and cooperative and competitive attitudes. Researchers tested 800 high school students over a period of 2 years, measuring their self-esteem via indicators such as their general sense of well-being, personal expressiveness, and conditionality of self-acceptance. Here, "conditionality of self-acceptance" refers to how much self-esteem depends on the approval of others. The researchers found that "students reporting positive attitudes towards competitive relationships with others are unique by virtue of their greater dependence on evaluation and performance-based assessments of personal worth" (Norem-Hebeisen & Johnson, 1981, p. 420). A competitive attitude may reflect personal insecurity rather than a "winning" self-image.

Competition Destroys Trust

If *trust* is defined as belief in both the reliability and benevolence of another, how, then, is it possible to trust a competitor? Why would you trust someone whose success depends upon your failure? Competition makes trusting an opponent's benign motives irrational. Intensifying this basis for mistrust is that competitive high stakes encourage people to cheat and play dirty (Kohn, 1986). Thus, it is reasonable to suspect that a competitor will not only act in ways to prevent you from reaching your goal, but may also engage in sneaky and unpredictable behaviors that violate rules of fair play. As introduced in Chapter 2, the theory of social interdependence confirms that trust is a casualty of competition (Johnson & Johnson, 2011). Breakdown of trust among team members impairs team performance (Levi, 2007). This is one of the reasons that within-group competition is a destructive dynamic in work groups and athletic teams.

Competition Elicits Envy

A complex emotion, envy is composed of other emotions such as discontent, ill will, and degrees of hatred (Cohen-Charash, 2009). It arises out of a sense of deprivation and the longing to have what someone else has, coupled with a competitive attitude. Competition is integral to envy (Ben-Ze'ev, 1990). One can wish for things that belong to another person and feel only admiration or selfless joy for their good fortune. But when the social comparison is combined with a competitive animus, the hostile and painful emotion of envy is at hand.

"Healthy Competition" Is an Oxymoron

Competition produces emotional stress (Gilbert, McEwan, Bellew, Mills, & Gale, 2009), which is potentially bad for one's mental and physical health in myriad ways. For example, consider the link between headaches and competition in children. The Health Encyclopedia of the University of Rochester Medical Center (2020) states that tension headaches, the most common type, "are almost always linked to stressful situations at school, *competition*, family friction, or excessive demands by parents."

Competition Discourages Sharing

Sharing is the joint use of resources or space as well as the process of dividing and distributing goods. Cooperation often involves sharing. Sharing is "pro-social" rather than "pro-self." Sharing bonds people together emotionally and nurtures love and friendship. It also helps keep deprivation at bay. When there is insufficient sharing in a community, resentment and desperation

justifiably build among have-nots, stoking misery, unrest, and the potential
for violence. Thus, sharing is as important on the scale of nations as it is
in a kindergarten sandbox. Nathan Ackerman, pioneer of family therapy,
wrote in 1958: "The strife of competition . . . impairs the mutuality of support and *sharing* and decreases the satisfaction of personal need" (quoted in
Kohn, 1986, p. 142). With a competitive mindset, we perceive scarcity even
when there is abundance. We battle for goods and hoard them rather than
share them and live in peace.

Competition Drives Cheating

In any competition, as we have learned, there are social rules for engagement that set boundaries as to what is fair. When the rules of fair play are
broken, it is called *cheating*. Though cheating is universally condemned as
unethical, it is also exceedingly common. When people cheat, they have
decided that winning is their priority, more pressing than the social com-
pact or even their own code of ethics. In a culture where winning is glori-
fied and "losers" are shamed, there can be significant temptation to win at
any cost, even by "playing dirty" (Kohn, 1986). In his 2007 article "Who's
Cheating Whom?," Kohn discusses reasons for cheating in school. There
are multiple causes for academic cheating, he explains, including excessive emphasis on measurable achievement and a curriculum so boring that
students have no real desire to learn it. But "a competitive school is to
cheating as a warm, moist environment is to mold," says Kohn (p. 91).
Competition intensifies the pressure to cheat because when one is publicly
ranked and judged accordingly, it's lonely and frightening to be named a
"loser."

Competition Intensifies Inequity

Anthropologist Margaret Mead observed the distribution of wealth in cultures around the world in her 1937 cross-cultural study, *Cooperation and
Competition Among Primitive Peoples.* She found that social goods are
distributed unevenly in cultures characterized by a high degree of competition; a much smaller gap exists between the rich and poor in cooperative
cultures. This makes logical sense. As explained earlier in the chapter, the
members of a group who possess the best resources at the outset of competition are most likely to win. As competition continues, those individuals with
the initial advantage continue to win preferentially. They therefore accumu-
late more resources and concentrate more advantage over time. Competition
thus assures that resources will continue to pile up for those members of the
group who had the initial advantage, and this of course intensifies the initial
inequity.

Competition Promotes Aggression

In competition, the resources competed for may be material (food, money, territory) or intangible (social status, power, or prestige.) In any case, because they introduce the possibility of loss, competitively structured social arrangements translate to a perception of threat. The perception of threat in turn triggers resentment, hostility, and a slew of aggression-inducing group dynamics. The theory of social interdependence, as introduced in Chapter 2, contemplates the escalation of hostility to aggression that is associated with competition. A massive amount of empirical evidence supporting the theory firmly establishes the link between them (Deutsch, 1949a; Johnson & Johnson, 2008). Much more is said about aggression as a grave downside of competition in Chapter 8.

Competition May Not Be Fun After All

Popular sports, games, and much other fun fare are structured competitively. For this reason, we associate competition with fun and enjoyment. Competition can undeniably be stimulating, but is it really fun? Competition characterizes many difficult, stressful circumstances such as legal battles, job searches, and lotteries. If competition itself were lots of fun, wouldn't we be smiling our way through these situations, too?

Terry Orlick, based on his research, suggests that the element of competition in recreational events is not what makes them fun. He showed that children often prefer cooperative games to competitive ones (Orlick, 1981). Perhaps it's not the element of competition but the atmosphere of celebration and community, zest and excitement, the sense of accomplishment, exercise, strategy, playfulness, and immersion in the moment that make traditional games, contests, and sports fun. The *I-win-if-you-lose-aspect* isn't what we enjoy after all.

Competition always produces losers. Losing a competition is surely not a fun experience, as downcast eyes, tears, and emotional meltdowns indicate. So when we say that we like to compete, is it because we are imagining the excitement of the winning experience? Is our professed enjoyment an accurate and balanced reflection of our total experience of competition? Or does it reflect a distorted view based on bias and selective memory that favors the winner's perspective?

Finally, is it possible that some of us, sometimes, enjoy competition because we like to fight? The popularity of gladiator games and blood sports in previous eras and the phenomenon of violent, competitive video games today would indicate that aggression itself can be fun for some people, sometimes. But when competition is enjoyed as an experience of aggression, is this form of "fun" something teachers and parents should encourage?

QUESTIONS FOR REFLECTION

3. Give an example of fun or entertainment that is not prosocial. Give an example of humor that is not prosocial.
4. Is it possible for a game to be challenging if it does not involve competition? If you said "yes," name an example.

HANDLING COMPETITION WITH CARE IN THE CLASSROOM

Given its many hazards, teachers are faced with the issue: "What is the best way to handle competition in my classroom?" Here are some options.

Teach the Topic of Competition

One approach is to directly teach the topic of competition—perhaps in the context of social-emotional learning, in connection with cooperative learning, or in the name of community building. Students can learn to be critical consumers of competition through experiential strategies such as games that are followed up with opportunities for reflection on hurt feelings and so on. Also, if students are old enough, they can learn about the social effects of competition by studying the theory of social interdependence. Once aware of its potential hazards and limitations, they can learn and devise strategies for competing in relatively healthy ways. This is guaranteed to be a high-interest topic that will spark engagement and debate! Of course, in class discussions, remember that competition is truly complex. The goal is to promote self-reflection and an appreciation for cooperation, rather than an intolerance for competition.

Young children can begin to understand the complexity of competition, too. I have found that children as young as kindergarten-age can be very articulate about their related feelings. It is common for children to experience emotional meltdowns when they lose. Gentle conversations about the downsides of competition can be therapeutic for students of any age.

Avoid Competition

Another response to the problems associated with competition in school, for example highly competitive games, is to simply avoid it. This is advocated in the Preschool Curriculum Framework of the California Department of Education (2013), which states: "Overly competitive games can work against community caring and collaborative learning and should be avoided." Generally speaking, the younger the students are, the less justification there is for competitive activities in the classroom. Young children need to develop trust, the ability to share, and the sense that they are free to follow through on what motivates them intrinsically. Competition undercuts these.

Allow Competition but Use Strategies to Reduce Risks

Another possible approach is to allow organized competition in class but to adopt strategies to mitigate the risks. For example, it is recommended that only modest rewards and prizes be given (Goldstein, 1999). The more valuable the rewards are in terms of prestige, material value, or grades, the more likely it is that the competition will elicit envy, anxiety, cheating, aggression, and all the rest. Keeping competition of short duration, frequently mixing up group membership, and stressing sportsmanship are other ways to moderate competition. You may wish to offer lighthearted competitive games occasionally for their excitement value. If so, you can tell students that it will be "game over" if you witness poor sportsmanship or other problems associated with competition. You may find it helpful to teach students what the negative social effects of competition are. They can then monitor themselves and learn to regulate their own behavior in competitive situations. This is a valuable life skill.

Use Cooperation as an Antidote to Excess Competition

Finally, it helps to counterbalance competition with cooperation. Give students plenty of exposure to cooperative and collaborative learning activities. These will build a cooperative classroom climate where antisocial expressions of competition are less likely to occur.

CHAPTER SUMMARY

Competition is an inherently adversarial arrangement because parties must work against each other in order to attain their own goals. Social interdependence theory, introduced in Chapter 2, has shown that competition is associated with negative social effects, including aggression. Given the risks and downsides, it is rather surprising that competition is so often exalted as a purely positive social force. In this chapter, some of the research and scholarship demonstrating the social and psychological downsides of competition is discussed. These effects include eliciting envy, stoking anxiety, intensifying inequity, destroying trust, provoking aggression, and more.

Various strategies can be used to minimize the potential harm associated with competition. These include offering only modest rewards and keeping competition of short duration. Cooperative games are also a powerful antidote. They set norms of cooperation and prompt critical examination of competition. The following chapter gives directions to a range of cooperative games that can be used to mitigate hurtful competition, and toward many other educational purposes as well.

PLAY TO LEARN—TRY THIS!

THUMB-WRESTLING TWO WAYS

Try this game to investigate assumptions about competition.

Directions:

1. Play with a partner. The goal is to thumb-wrestle and pin your partner's thumb as frequently as you can in one minute (Figure 3.1). Look at a clock and be ready to count. Ready-set-go.
2. Done? Who won? How many pins did each partner score?
3. You played the competitive game, now play the cooperative one. Thumb-wrestle with the same goal—each partner aims to score as many points as they can. But this time, partners cooperate by taking turns pinning thumbs in a coordinated and efficient way. How many points do you score now? Ready, set, go!
4. Compare points when you cooperated versus when you competed.

Figure 3.1. Thumb-Wrestling Two Ways helps students learn through direct experience that cooperation can be an efficient way to win, even when self-interest is the only motivator.

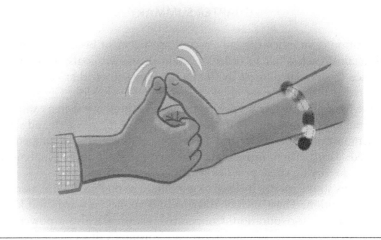

Part II

SOME COOPERATIVE GAMES AND GUIDELINES FOR PRACTICE

CHAPTER 4

A Gallery of Cooperative Games

Do not keep children to their studies by compulsion but by play.

—Plato

One of the first cooperative games I created was *Cooperative Musical Chairs*. The way I changed this game from its original competitive design illustrates a basic difference between cooperative games and competitive games . . . Each time the music plays in competitive *Musical Chairs*, another chair is removed, and another child is eliminated . . . until one child—the winner—is left on the chair and all the others are left out sitting on the sidelines . . . I have watched young children play the competitive version of *Musical Chairs* on many occasions and witnessed their tears and looks of despair as each one is eliminated from the game . . . The game is designed to eliminate children by ensuring that they do not find a chair. Games of elimination are totally inappropriate for young children. Children need games of inclusion, not games of rejection.

—Terry Orlick (2006, pp. 21-22)

This chapter presents a collection of cooperative games for children from pre-K to high school, including Terry Orlick's Cooperative Musical Chairs mentioned above. (Directions to it are provided in the "Play to Learn" section at the end of this chapter.) I have attributed credit to the authors of these games where I could, though the ultimate source of some of the games is uncertain. In some cases I have adapted games to better suit school settings or for some other purpose. Some of the games were designed by me. Notice that there are a variety of different types of games gathered here. I have grouped them under representative headings even though some games fit multiple categories. Always feel free to invent, modify, and personalize. Enjoy!

COOPERATIVE GAMES FOR WELCOMING AND INCLUSION

Toss a Name

The group stands in a circle. Everyone says their own name, one at a time, going all the way around. Next, a ball is introduced to the group. The player holding the ball says her name, then throws it to someone else while saying his name, like this: "My name is Rhonda and this is Lee." Lee repeats the pattern, saying his name and throwing the ball to someone else while saying her name. The game is over when everyone has had a chance to catch the ball and pass it on. The only rule is that no name can be called twice.

Variations:

Go around the circle multiple times or use multiple balls at the same time.

Zoom Hello

This is like Toss a Name but it is played in online settings, such as in Zoom meetings. It is a way of bringing the group together and making the experience more social. First, ask all attendees to use the gallery view function so players can see one another. The facilitator ("Nadine") tosses an imaginary ball to someone she randomly chooses ("AJ") while saying "My name is Nadine, and this is AJ." AJ then has the ball, says his own name, and throws the ball to someone else, whose name he says. The ball is tossed virtually around the group until everyone has been welcomed into the meeting. The playful part of this is the pretend tossing of the ball.

Sharing Highlights

The group gathers in a circle. Each person has a chance to share a *highlight*—a positive experience. Prompts that provide focus include, "Tell us one thing that made you feel proud yesterday or today" and "What has been the best part of your day so far?"

Variations:

1. This game is easily adapted to online forums. Players type their highlight into the chat feature. The moderator or a helper reads highlights to the group.
2. Players can draw pictures of their highlights, describe them in writing, or bring in photos.
3. Players can act out their highlights for a partner or small group to guess. This is Highlights Charades.

4. Highlight Our Friend is like the first version except that players name something they respect, love, or admire about a particular member of the group. This is a nice way to celebrate birthdays! (Adapted from Orlick, 2006)

Find Your Type

Preparation:

Make pairs of $3'' \times 5''$ cards with the same animal on each pair. You will need one card for each student.

Directions:

Get the group into a circle. Distribute one card to each student and tell them to find their mates by doing something the animal would do. Goofy animal imitations allowed! No talking, though. Ready, set, go!

The Name Game

The group is arranged in a circle. Individual players think of an adjective describing themselves or how they feel that begins with the same letter as their name, for example, "Silly Suzanne." The players each introduce themselves this way (Fletcher & Kunst, 2006).

Variation:

Make it a memory challenge game so that the players not only say their own name and adjective but repeat the name and adjective of every player who has gone before in the circle. Cooperative assistance will likely be needed for large groups!

Parachute Popcorn

Parachute play is a staple form of cooperative play. Parachutes are dramatic to look at and play with and add a sense of celebration. Parachute Popcorn is a lively and simple game: Gather enough participants around the parachute to hold it firmly. Roll lightweight objects such as beach balls or rolled-up socks onto the parachute. Start the "popcorn" popping by shaking the parachute up and down in unison. See how high the "kernels" can fly out of the "pan." It is fun to pop real popcorn in a skillet (and eat it!) before the game to be sure everyone understands the reference (adapted from Orlick, 1982).

QUESTION FOR REFLECTION

1. Which of the preceding games would you like to try? Why?

COOPERATIVE GAMES FOR TRUST-BUILDING
AND EMPATHY

Partner Walk

This is a trust-building game. It can be played outside or inside in an area where there are obstacles to walk around. Divide the class into pairs. One child from each pair wears a blindfold. The partners hook arms. The one who can see leads the blindfolded partner safely around the obstacles, silently helping his partner avoid them.

Feeling Mirror

Cut a piece of cardboard into the shape of a frame about 2 feet on each side. Children sit in a circle. Tell them, "Hold the frame up to your face, make an emotional face, and name the emotion. For example, say 'This is a mad face.'" Repeat with different emotions such as happy, sad, scared, proud, disappointed, excited, and so forth.

Variation:

Children sit in a circle. One child makes a feeling face and names it, and the child next to him mirrors it. Then the second child does the same thing with a new feeling face with the child on her other side. Go around the circle this way until everyone has had the chance to mirror the feeling face of their neighbor and make a new feeling face to pass on.

Mirroring Technique

Children work in pairs. Facing each other, one child makes interesting movements while the other tries to exactly mimic her, as if he is her mirror image. The pairs have a few minutes to practice their movement routine, then the class comes back together. Each pair now shows their movement routine to the class. The class tries to guess which partner is the leader and who is the "reflection" (Deranja, 2004).

Caterpillar

Students lie facedown on the carpet or rubber mats. They squeeze together as closely as possible. The player at the end tucks in his arms and rolls over the backs of the other players. When he reaches the other end of the lineup, he lies down next to the end student. The next child at the end then rolls over the students. The game is over when the "caterpillar" runs out of room, for example by running into a wall. This game is most appropriate for very young children.

Back-to-Back

This game can be played inside or outside on a soft surface. Children count off to form partners. Partners stand back-to-back, pressing their backs together. They try to sit down slowly, remaining in position without using their hands or toppling over. Once seated, they try to stand back up remaining back-to-back.

COOPERATIVE GAMES FOR COMMUNITY-BUILDING

Common Ground

Students sit in chairs arranged in a circle, while one person stands in the middle to become the caller. The caller says, "I seek common ground with [everyone who had cereal for breakfast, is wearing blue shoes, has a pet bird, etc.]." Anyone seated in the circle who fits the category must get up and stand in the center, hold hands with the others, or take a bow in unison at the behest of the caller. Next, on a count of 3, players inside the circle disperse, running to get a seat. However, they cannot return to the seat they came from. At the end of the scramble, there will be one person left without a seat who goes to the middle of the circle, becomes the next caller, and makes the next request.

Variation:

Use meaningful criteria so that players discover others with significant things in common. This can potentially bridge divides and show that sometimes folks have more in common than they know. For example, "I seek common ground with everyone who has ever had a pet adopted from an animal shelter." In expert hands, this game can be used to treat trauma. For example, it has been used therapeutically in prisons among inmates. By joining others in the circle, participants can see they are not the only ones who have suffered from the trauma that the caller has identified.

Clap Happy

Students assemble as a group. A volunteer leaves the group while those remaining decide on a gesture or position that the volunteer should strike. For example, the group may decide that the volunteer should salute or touch her toes. When the volunteer returns to the group, she randomly strikes different poses. As she gets "warmer," the group claps louder and more frequently until clapping reaches a crescendo as the correct pose is reached.

Personal Best

Students run a certain distance while a timekeeper records how long it takes. At a later date, students repeat. Everyone wins whose 2nd time is an improvement compared to baseline (Lyons, 2021). In postgame reflection, ask students how it feels to "lose" when "competing" against oneself versus losing to someone else. For most people, it's not disappointment in one's performance that hurts most; rather, it's the experience of being "worse than" and "bested" by someone else.

Pass the Funny Face

Students sit in a circle. One child starts the game by turning to his neighbor to the left and making a funny face. He then turns to his neighbor on the right and makes a different funny face. Players on both sides mimic the funny face passed to them. Continue playing until the two funny faces have reached the initial player or laughter has stopped the game (Harrison, 1975).

Cooperative Trains

Begin the game by forming 2-person trains that chug around the play area. Players maintain contact by keeping both hands on the hips or shoulders of the person in front of them. Little trains link together to make bigger trains until there is one big train moving in unison. Chug around the entire play zone, snaking around obstacles. Expect lots of laughing and sound effects, "choo-choo!"

COOPERATIVE GAMES TO PREVENT BULLYING

The games in this category were used in the 1994 University of Nevada, Reno study by Bay-Hinitz et al., mentioned in the Introduction and Chapter 2. These games, in combination with the others tested, increased prosocial behavior and decreased aggression. More information on this study and the games shown to prevent bullying can be found in Chapter 8.

Balance Activities

Gather materials: a large rubber ball and other objects that can be balanced between partners such as oranges or yoga blocks. To play: Players put the ball between their bodies (for example, tummy to tummy) and try to prevent it from falling to the floor. When they have mastered this, they try the other objects. Students cannot use their hands to keep the object balanced between them. They can hold hands, or they can keep hands at their sides.

Cooperative Musical Hugs

At least 8 players are needed for this active game. To begin, play lively music to get children energized and moving around the play area. Unexpectedly, stop the music. Players quickly team up with someone to hug. Resume the music. The children begin dancing around to the music, now with their partner. Stop the music again. Now at least three children hug together. Continue starting and stopping the music. Each time it stops, each hugging huddle adds one more person, and when the music begins, the huddle moves together (Orlick, 2006).

Freeze DeFreeze Tag

In this game of tag, a few children will be the *freezers*. The object of the game is to freeze your friends if you are a freezer, and thaw frozen friends if you are not a freezer. To begin, freezers count to 10 while the rest of the children scatter about. After 10 seconds the running begins. Freezers set off after the runners and try to tag them. When a child is tagged, he becomes frozen in a stride position with one arm outstretched. The runners attempt to thaw their frozen friends by shaking their hands or passing under their legs. To keep the game moving at the right pace so thawing and freezing are both occurring, you can add or subtract more freezers by calling names. The game is over when the group is tired and ready to quit (Orlick, 2006).

Devine

This game is named for the French word *deviner*, which means "guess." You will need a sheet or blanket and a mystery object that should be interesting to handle. For example, it could be a peeled grape or a sponge. Invite children to sit in the circle. Spread the sheet in the center of the circle so it overlaps hands and forearms. The students pass the mystery object from one to another under the sheet without looking at it. After everyone has had a chance to feel the object, children guess what it is (Orlick, 1982).

Half a Heart

First, you will need to make some materials for this game. Use red construction paper. Draw heart shapes that are at least 3 inches tall. You will need half as many hearts as you have children playing the game. On one half of each heart, write a number with a thick marker. On the other side, draw that number of dots. Cut the hearts in half so one side has the number and the other side has the dots (Figure 4.1).

Figure 4.1. Each heart has a number on one side and a corresponding number of dots on the other side.

Now, give each child half a heart. Ask the children to skip around the room while you play some music. Now, stop the music. Children compare hearts and find their match. Pairs sit together, building a circle including the whole class (Orlick, 1978).

COOPERATIVE GAMES FOR YOUNG CHILDREN

Up in the Air

This game works for 6 or more players. Children sit on the ground, spreading out so they are about arm's-length away from one another. The object of the game is to tap a beachball to keep it in the air while remaining seated on the ground. It's a win if all players touch the ball once, and no one has touched it more than once.

Balloon Bop

This is a lot like Up in the Air, but there are a few differences. Children congregate in groups of 5 to 10, standing a few feet apart. They pass the balloon from one to another by tapping it with their hands. The goal is for everyone in the group to bop it once and not let the balloon hit the ground. Subsequent rounds are played with other body parts: bopping the balloon with elbows, heads, shoulders, feet, and so on (Orlick, 1978).

Cooperative Pin the Tail on the Donkey

Play the traditional party game: Spin a blindfolded child and send him off to find the donkey. He then tries to "pin" (that is, tape) the tail on the donkey's behind where it belongs, but it is likely to end up elsewhere. In the cooperative version, the blindfolded child gets guidance from the on-looking crowd, who shout "higher," "lower," "turn around," and so forth. It is still okay for the crowd to giggle as their classmate gropes for the donkey's rump, but now they can offer help (Orlick, 2006).

No-Elimination Simon Says

Two groups of children play Simon Says in parallel. If a player follows what the leader does but the leader has not said "Simon Says," the player is not eliminated. Instead, he runs over to the other team and joins their game (Orlick, 2006).

Everybody's It

Children play tag as in the traditional game, but in this version every child tries to gently tag as many others as they can. Game runs for 5 minutes.

London Bridge Is Falling Down

This classic nursery school game is quite cooperative. Children form parallel lines and face each other. Each facing pair clasps hands with each other over their heads to form a bridge. Children break off the end of the line one by one and run under the bridge while the group sings the following song:

> *London Bridge is falling down, falling down, falling down.*
> *London Bridge is falling down, my fair lady.*
> *Build it up with silver and gold, silver and gold, silver and gold.*
> *Build it up with silver and gold, my fair LADY.*

The bridge falls down—hands come down and catch the child running through—on the last word of the song ("LADY").

Giant Animals

Children play together to turn their bodies into different parts of a giant animal. To begin, each group of four to six students decides on a different animal to create. Each child selects a different body part to be. Then the group assembles and tries to make the animal. Once the animal is assembled, they try to get it moving—rolling over, jumping, stretching, wagging its tail, and so on. If you have a large class with lots of animals, you can make a giant animal zoo! (Orlick, 2006).

Variations:

Make a giant monster, giant space alien, or giant flower.

QUESTION FOR REFLECTION

2. Cooperatively structured games are not a new phenomenon, especially in early childhood education. In what sense are cooperative games a social innovation? Give an example of a traditional cooperative game and an innovative cooperative game.

COOPERATIVE GAMES FOR OLDER CHILDREN, TWEENS, AND TEENS

Twenty Questions

One player thinks of an animal, food, or object found at school. She tells other players what category the mystery item belongs to. Players pair up and formulate a yes-no question to guess the item. Each pair takes a turn guessing. After 20 questions, if the item has not been guessed, the questioners get one more turn. Otherwise, another volunteer gets to ask the next question.

People to People

An odd number of players is needed. Children form pairs and face each other. The odd-numbered player stands at the end of the line and is the first caller. The caller yells "toe to toe," "hand to hand," "pinky to pinky," and so forth, and each pair connects their body parts accordingly each time. On the call "people to people," players switch partners. To do this, one of the lines of players shifts left or right. This shift gives the first caller a partner and produces a new odd player who becomes the next caller (Fletcher & Kunst, 2006).

Quick-Change Artist

Players form pairs and stand face-to-face. They look at one another for one minute, then turn away so they cannot see one another. They have another minute to change something about their appearance such as zipping a sweater or untying a shoe. They make as many changes as they have time for. Partners face each other and try to guess what changes were made.

Sardines

This is the cooperative version of Hide and Seek. The player who is "It" hides first. Then everyone tries to find "It." When someone does, that player hides in the same spot along with "It." The game is over when everyone huddles together in the hiding spot—like sardines.

People Chairs

Players begin by standing in a circle and holding hands. On the caller's cue, players let go of hands and make a quarter turn to the right. Now, everyone's left shoulder points directly toward the center of the circle. Every player is looking at the back of the player in front of them. Be sure the circle is tight. Caller counts to 3 and everyone bends their knees. Everyone sits on the knees of the player behind them and holds the shoulders of the player in front of them. Practice the game several times. The goal is to make it a coordinated event, with everyone sitting down on a neighbor's knees securely and in sync.

COOPERATIVE GAMES TO TEACH LANGUAGE ARTS

Cooperative Alphabet (Prereading)

Distribute big cards with letters of the alphabet on them. Ask children to line up in order without talking, assembling the alphabet. Children are encouraged to help one another, but no words can be exchanged.

Cooperative Alphabet (Spelling and Reading Practice)

This game is like the previous one, where kids line up in alphabetical order. But in this version, kids each choose a card with a picture on it. The pictures show items beginning with each letter of the alphabet, but the words are not spelled out. (For example, "A" is represented by a picture of an apple not accompanied by the word "apple.") Again, children are encouraged to help one another get into line, but no words can be exchanged.

Infinite Story

Make a story as a group. Each person adds a sentence or two that takes off from where the person before them left the story. The game is over when everyone has had a chance (or two or three chances, etc.) to contribute. Note: You may want to start the group off by providing the first part of the story. Special occasions can make good story beginnings. For example, on Halloween, begin a story about a black cat wandering into a schoolyard.

Fortunately, Unfortunately

This game is like Infinite Story described above, except in this case, players begin their part of the story either with the word "fortunately" or "unfortunately." They then proceed to tell a fortunate or unfortunate development in the story line. The fortunate and unfortunate parts of the story alternate; for example:

> *Player 1: Unfortunately,* when the man crossed the street he stepped on a banana peel.
> *Player 2: Fortunately,* he didn't fall when he stepped on the peel.
> *Player 3: Unfortunately,* the man skated on the banana peel all the way across the street.
> *Player 4: Fortunately,* there were no cars driving on the street at that time.
> *Player 5: Unfortunately,* the man crashed into an ice cream cart parked along the curb.
> *Player 6: Fortunately,* the man crashed into an ice cream cone and got to taste the best vanilla ice cream he ever had (Deranja, 2004).

COOPERATIVE GAMES TO TEACH MATH

Human Number Line

This game involves sequencing. It can be adapted to decimals, fractions, integers, and so on. Give each student a large card with a number on it. The students self-assemble in numerical order without talking. For more fun, have kids play against a timer so they have to scramble quickly into line.

Variation:

Play this game with positive and negative integers such that pairs of kids choose to be the positive and negative side of 1, 2, 3, and so on. Kids should catch on quickly that they need to position themselves symmetrically around the "0" card to build a number line of all the integers.

Sequences

Using a standard deck of cards, this card game for 2 to 10 players sharpens computational skills. The goal is for each player to have her entire hand in a run—any suits are okay, but numbers must be in a consecutive order. Deal cards equally among players. All players arrange their cards in a hand. Then all players call out a desired number, a number they need for a run. After the call, each player passes one of her cards to the left. If she has the number desired by the person to her left, she passes that card. If not, she passes another that someone else has called out, with the hope that it will soon reach the party who desired it. Next, there is another call for desired numbers, and another passing of cards to the left. When any player has four or more cards in sequence, she places the cards on the table in front of her. She keeps adding cards to the run as she gets them. The game is won when all players have all cards in sequences. (Before the game is begun, players can agree on the number of turns they will allow themselves to complete the game.)

Shape It Up

For background, describe geometric shapes and show pictures of them. Divide students into small groups. Then, name a particular shape and ask each group of students to form that shape with their bodies. It is easiest to start with a circle, then move on to square, rectangle, triangle, oval, octagon, half-circle, and so on.

QUESTION FOR REFLECTION

3. Adapt the game Human Number Line to create a game that teaches another subject. Use the same basic game mechanics.

COOPERATIVE GAMES TO TEACH SCIENCE

Human Circuit

The class, including you, the teacher, stands in a circle holding hands. Squeeze the hand of the student on your left, who passes it on to their neighbor to their left, who then passes it on to their left, all the way around the circle. The pulse travels around the circle like an electrical current in a circuit.

The Story of Science

Science content can be viewed as a narrative, a story. So have your students assemble in a circle and tell a science story, chapter upon chapter. If someone forgets part of the narrative, others chime in to help. This game can be used as a review at the end of a unit. For example, if a middle school earth science class just studied plate tectonics, the first student can begin the story with Wegener's hypothesis of continental drift. The final part of the story could be the discovery of magnetic stripes. Younger students could create a science story centered on the topic of pollination. Players add bees, butterflies, fruit, flowers, grocery stores, and people in sequence to the unfolding story (Lyons, 2021).

Webbing

This game models the interdependence of biotic and abiotic components of an ecosystem. Children stand in a circle, preferably outside. The leader stands close to the edge of the circle with a ball of string. The leader asks questions and responds to answers in a storytelling fashion such as this:

> *Leader:* Who can name a plant that grows in this area?
> *Student:* Brodiaea does.
> *Leader:* Good. Here, Miss Brodiaea, you hold the end of the string. Now, is there an animal living around here that might eat Brodiaea?
> *Student:* Rabbits.
> *Leader:* Ah, a sumptuous meal. Mr. Rabbit, you take hold of the string here. You are connected to Miss Brodiaea by your dependence on her flowers for your lunch. Now, who needs Mr. Rabbit for his lunch?

The leader continues to connect the children with string as their relationships to the rest of the group are stated. The leader brings in new elements and connections such as other animals, soil, water, and so on, until the entire circle of children is strung together in a symbol of the web of life. To demonstrate how each individual is important to the community, the leader takes away one member of the web by some plausible means. For example, a logger kills a "tree." When the "tree" actually falls down, it tugs on the strings it holds; anyone who feels a tug on the string is in some way affected by the death of the tree. Next, everyone who felt a tug from the tree gives a tug. The process continues until every individual is shown to be affected by the destruction of the tree. (From J. Cornell, *Sharing Nature With Children*, 20th Anniversary Edition (pp. 60–61), 1998, Sharing Nature Worldwide, © 1998 by Sharing Nature Worldwide. Reprinted with permission.)

Coral Reef

Children do research and make model fish (or cut out pictures) that inhabit coral reefs and then attach them to a make-believe coral reef. When the reef is finished, children mill around it, pretending to be swimming fish. When you give the cue, they "swim" to the reef, and all try to touch it without touching one another. See how many fishes can squeeze together yet avoid touching (Lyons, 2015).

Reconciliation Ecology: Win-Win Thinking for Ecosystems

This game is based on the biodiversity conservation model articulated by University of Arizona ecology professor Michael L. Rosenzweig in his book *Win-Win Ecology: How the Earth's Species Can Survive in the Midst of Human Enterprise* (2003). Rosenzweig's approach is named *reconciliation ecology*. What does it entail? Reconciliation ecology "is the science of inventing, establishing, and maintaining new habitats to conserve species diversity in places where people live, work, and play" (Rosenzweig, 2003, p. 7).

To play this game, students build an ecosystem that demonstrates the principles of reconciliation ecology. They begin seated in a circle. As a group, they agree upon an ecosystem inhabited by humans to work with. They diagram it—however simply or elaborately they wish—on the chalkboard, a piece of paper, and so on. Next, students take turns naming a species that can be sustainably introduced to this environment. Players use books and other resources and can help one another on each of their turns. Each species gets added to the diagram once the group agrees it was correctly chosen. The group as a whole wins if a new species can be identified on each player's turn (Lyons, 2021).

CLASSIC COOPERATIVE PLAY ACTIVITIES

Making quilts; painting murals; producing puppet shows; staging plays, recitals, and skits; building with blocks; assembling puzzles; creating playhouses from empty cardboard boxes; playing house or catch; jumping rope; playing peekaboo; dancing and singing together; spinning a merry-go-round; sledding and building snowmen; riding a tandem bike; having a tea party; dramatic play with dolls and toy figures; riding seesaws up and down.

CHAPTER SUMMARY

Chapter 4 is a collection of cooperative games and activities for students of all ages. Identifying games to serve your educational objectives is only half of the teaching task, however. What students learn from the game experience depends largely on the teaching strategies you use as well. The next chapter will show you how to facilitate cooperative games in an expert way to fully tap their educational potential.

PLAY TO LEARN—TRY THIS!

COOPERATIVE MUSICAL CHAIRS

Directions:

Play musical chairs as in the traditional game, but when the music stops, remove a chair rather than a player. With every round another chair is removed. The group wins as a whole if they manage to all sit on the last chair or on someone's lap who is sitting on that chair (Figure 4.2). If this is physically impossible due to the number of players, huddling together so everyone is touching is also a win (Orlick, 2006).

Figure 4.2. Cooperative Musical Chairs, a classic active cooperative game created by Terry Orlick, Ph.D.

A Guide to Facilitating Cooperative Games

Frame your mind to mirth and merriment
Which bars a thousand harms
And lengthens life.

—*William Shakespeare*, The Taming of the Shrew

> I was sitting outside the conference room waiting to give a workshop for teachers. A teacher from the audience was hanging out there, too. She was taking a breather from the talk. She told me she had to leave the conference because the slide presentation was boring her to tears! She said that she and her colleagues were all teachers, and like their students, "we learn best through play." Looking at the room, I saw the teachers were indeed drooping in their seats with glazed expressions. In that moment, I decided to ditch the lecture-based presentation I had planned. Instead, we would start by playing cooperative games. Only after everyone was revitalized would we get to intellectual part of the talk. The change was easy to make on the spot. The teachers sprang to life and stayed alert and engaged for the next 90 minutes. Now I always start presentations with cooperative games. I don't think there is any better way to get a group excited and ready to learn.
>
> Author at a workshop sponsored by the Alameda County, CA, Office of Education, 2018

A skilled facilitator uses cooperative games with purpose, flexibility, and confidence. Your skill as facilitator will develop over time. Even if you are brand-new to the practice, though, you are likely to have good results if you keep a few basic guidelines in mind. This chapter will begin by giving you these basic guidelines for facilitating games. I then provide pointers for designing educational cooperative games yourself. Last but not least, you will learn strategies for converting traditional competitive games to cooperative ones.

THE FIVE STEPS OF FACILITATING GAMES

Generally speaking, there are five basic steps to follow whenever you use cooperative games for an educational purpose. Here are the five steps:

1. Choose a good game.
2. Take care of logistics.
3. Frame the game.
4. Lead the game.
5. Guide reflection.

We will consider each of these steps in detail.

1. Choose a Good Game

What purpose are you using cooperative games for? Will you be supporting cooperative learning, teaching academic subjects, trying to prevent bullying, or something else? Once you are clear on your purpose, you can find suitable games in this or other books or on websites. Or you can make games up yourself. Select games according to the following criteria:

- *Age and Development Level:* Are the games you have in mind developmentally appropriate for your group? Cooperative play activities and simple group games work best for preschoolers; kindergarten and "TK" (transition to kindergarten) children can play games with rules; children in the primary grades are developing the cognitive capacity for strategy games. Middle-schoolers like to be silly and are highly peer-focused, so big group games are good for them. Teens and adults enjoy games that foster deep communication and personal intimacy as well intellectual stimulation.
- *Run Time:* Can the game be completed in the time allowed?
- *Materials:* Will the required materials be available to you?
- *Quality:* Screen games for quality. Be sure a proposed game has the four essential features of all good cooperative games: cooperation, inclusion, acceptance, and fun (Orlick, 2006).
- *Equity and Inclusion:* The defining rules of cooperative games inherently promote equity and inclusion, but the way you facilitate them is crucial as well. Apply what you know about equitable, developmentally appropriate, and culturally responsive practice. When it comes to choosing games with equity in mind, ask yourself if they are accessible to your students. Can the game be adapted to include children with physical or mental differences? Can you use the game in a way that is aligned with trauma-informed practice? Is the game free of narratives that echo cultural oppression? Does

the game storyline instead celebrate good things like peace, fun everyday life topics, and cultural diversity? Are you introducing a variety of games so that the different strengths and preferences of all students all have time in the spotlight? Give yourself the time and self-care that it takes to turn off the internal pressure to hurry through your planning and preparation.

QUESTION FOR REFLECTION

1. Describe a cooperative game that you think would be a good choice for 1) preschool students, 2) middle-school students, and 3) college students. Explain why you think each of these games is a good choice.

---

2. Take Care of Logistics

This is the preparation piece. Gather materials and take care of any specific preparation needed. Here are some logistical issues to consider.

- *The Game Space*: Where will you play the game—in the classroom, playground, gymnasium, or somewhere else? Consider designating a play zone for active games, a place where the children will gather when you announce it is time to play. To establish a play zone, use mats to define an area of your classroom. Or make a circle with colored tape or put a rug in a corner of the room, playground, or gym. Or you might draw a fun shape on the playground with chalk, among other ways. Be sure to have plenty of room for active games. Choose a cozy space for quiet circle games where talking and listening are important.
- *Understand the Directions*: Because you will need to explain the game directions clearly, you will need to understand them thoroughly before engaging your class. Ideally, you should practice the game before you present it to your students to play.
- *Set Up for Board Games*: If you will be using board games, consider stationing different games in various locations around the room. Players can rotate among them. If you are using only a single game but have many players, you may want to invest in several copies of the game. Card games are a good alternative to board games for larger groups.
- *Organize Volunteers*: It's great to have volunteers on hand, especially for running complex games or several games at once. Volunteers can also help by assisting children with special needs who may require a little extra attention and support. Also,

parents, students from older grades, and colleagues—especially the principal—add excitement. Be sure to meet with volunteers before class to explain specifically how they can assist you. In Chapter 8, I discuss *cooperative contact*, which is contact that facilitates improved relations among people from adversarial groups (Allport, 1954). Research has shown that the effectiveness of any particular method of cooperative contact will be enhanced if leaders and authorities explicitly endorse that method (Goldstein, 2002). So if administrators and fellow teachers show their support of cooperative games, the games will likely be even better at healing social divisions and fostering kindness among your students.

- *Sequence Games Properly*: Are you running a series of games? If so, think about how to sequence them for best effect. Games that introduce players, such as Toss a Name, are handy for introductions. (Directions for all games mentioned in this chapter can be found in Chapter 4.) It is best to delay playing games that involve physical closeness until after the group has participated in other games that have helped to soften the personal space bubble. Likewise, it is best to save complex games until simpler ones have proven successful.

- *Consider Trauma-Sensitive Practice:* Two-thirds of children age 16 and under have suffered from at least one traumatic event (Copeland, Keeler, Angold, & Costello, 2007). Trauma can abnormally activate a child's stress response system so that she feels threatened even in objectively safe situations. With her brain bathed in stress hormones, she remains on high alert, is agitated, and cannot access the higher levels of brain function associated with learning and reason. The *neurosequential model of education* (NME) provides brain-based guidance for educating children who are victims of toxic stress and trauma. According to the NME, academic work should be preceded by two kinds of activities that help students regulate their stress response (Rizzi, 2021). First, calming and breathing exercises should be used to regulate the involuntary nervous system. Next, activities that help children feel relationally safe should be used to mitigate emotional distress rooted in maltreatment and traumatic interpersonal experiences. Gentle cooperative games are a good choice for this part of the treatment due to their positive social effects (Orlick, 1983). Please see examples from Chapter 4.

- *Consider Students Who Opt Out:* Have a plan for students who do not want to join whole-class games. Remember that play, by definition, must be freely chosen. So do not force children to participate. Do encourage them to watch the game, though. Once onlookers see that the game is fun, that their peers are welcoming, and that they will be able to perform satisfactorily, they are likely to join. Keep inviting them in, and don't give up! The students who are most hesitant to play are often the ones who will benefit most. If, however, circumstances dictate it, you can provide an alternate activity. Perhaps allow students to read a book or work on class assignments as a replacement for the game.

- *Safety Check:* Evaluate any risks inherent in the game and setting. Take proper precautions. Falling and tripping are common concerns. Do not use small game parts that present a choking hazard for young children.

3. Frame the Game

You will want to frame the game to set the mood, convey the rules, and pique excitement prior to play. Here are some framing tips and techniques.

- *Discuss the Words* Cooperation *and* Competition*:* In my experience, children of kindergarten age often understand that there is a big difference in how cooperation and competition make them feel. Draw this out through dialogue. Ask, "How do you feel when you cooperate with someone? When you compete?" Be sure not to judge, lecture, or shame anyone who has positive things to say about competition. Mainly encourage students to reflect on an important phenomenon that is rarely discussed—the social and emotional effects of cooperation versus competition.
- *Remind Students of the Cooperative Intention:* If necessary, remind students that the intention is playing together and having fun as a group rather than winning as an individual.
- *Tell a Story:* It can be fun to lead the students on an imaginary journey where cooperation is the key to survival or success. For example, before playing Cooperative Musical Chairs, tell students to imagine they are at the beach. Anyone not clinging to the rock (actually, the last remaining chair) when the water rises will be washed away!
- *Give Hints:* Prime students about what to look for in the game experience. For example, ask players to notice how much attentive listening is occurring; how inclusive the game is; how encouraging players are; and so on.
- *Models and Metaphors:* Older students may be able to see games as metaphors or models for larger social phenomena. Encourage them to do so with prompts such as: "When you play this game, consider how it models democracy."
- *Discuss Social Skills:* If you are trying to teach any particular social skills, such as encouraging or helping others, discuss them in advance of the game. Tell students to monitor the game and look for that social skill in action (Cohen, 1986). You may wish to keep a tally.

- *Discuss Special Intentions:* If you have a special purpose in mind for the game, for example learning students' names, now is the time to express it.

4. Lead the Game

This part is the most fun for everyone. Here are a few pointers.

- *Give Directions:* Gather students close in so they can all hear and see you clearly. Ask young students to maintain eye contact while you are talking. State directions as simply as you can. You might want to call up a volunteer from the group to help you demonstrate steps of the game. If children can read, list game rules on the chalkboard or on a poster.
- *Establish a Pay-Attention Signal:* Have a signal that tells students to stop playing and look at you. Common methods include holding up five fingers, clapping hands, banging a tambourine, and blowing a whistle. Such a signal will be helpful if you want to change game rules, announce that the game is almost over, and so on.
- *Introduce Volunteers:* Explain the role of any volunteers who are present.
- *Discuss Safety:* Emphasize safety precautions before you begin the game.
- *Participate in the Game:* It is time to get started. If you like, play alongside your students. Being embedded in the game puts you in a good position to assess how it is working.
- *Observe Closely:* Is everyone participating? Does everyone look engaged? Monitor and assist as needed.
- *Be Flexible:* If children are confused or the game is not running smoothly, try to figure out what is going on. You might want to change rules or reduce the challenge to maximize the fun.
- *End Games When Everyone Is Tired:* Do not let games go on too long. If the students are tired and everyone has had their opportunity to participate, it is time to call it a day.
- *Regroup Between Consecutive Games:* After one game you may wish to start another. Refocus the group by giving them the signal to pay attention. Then ask them to freeze, drop to one knee, take a seat, or return to the play zone while you explain the next set of rules.
- *No Elimination:* If students are disruptive, find a way to focus their attention back on the game. The only reason to eliminate a player from the game is if he deliberately tries to physically hurt someone else. If this happens, do not hesitate to remove the player right away. Explain to him that violence is never allowed. Tell him you hope that he will be able to come back to the group soon. Maintain a calm and caring mindset, but be firm.

5. Guide Reflection

Once the game is ended, postgame reflection takes place. Reflection is both a process of self-reflection and a group processing experience. Through reflection, students draw personally meaningful lessons from their experience. They also have the chance to talk with one another about how well they functioned as a cooperative group, and what they might do better next time. Reflection can also give the facilitator important feedback for improving the game. Reflection typically consists of whole-class discussion. It is helpful to have a note-taker. The following types of questions work well (Fletcher & Kunst, 2006):

- *Open-Ended Questions:* For example, ask, "What did you learn about yourself by playing this game?" and "What is enjoyable about this game?" Such questions promote thoughtful discussion and participation.
- *Feeling Questions:* Ask questions such as, "How did you feel when you replaced the beanbag on your friend's head?" and "How did you feel when all your friends donated points so you would not be left out of the game?" If the group is a supportive and inclusive one, students are likely to respond to feeling questions in ways that express trust and caring. Feelings of caring, community, and intimacy may become palpable.
- *Judgment Questions:* Players make evaluations and comparisons about their experience. Good judgment questions include, "Would you recommend this game to your younger sister?" and "Was this one of your favorite games?"
- *Philosophical Questions:* Ask such questions to help students relate the game to bigger issues beyond it. Philosophical questions include, "How do the cooperative skills you practiced in this game help people in their lives?" and "Is it better to win as an individual or as part of a group? Why do you think so?"
- *Closing Questions:* These questions help wrap up the experience. Good closing questions are "How would you change this game next time you play?" and "What was your favorite part of the game?"

QUESTION FOR REFLECTION

2. Imagine that your students have just played a game of Cooperative Musical Chairs. State five good postgame reflection questions, one from each category above.

DESIGNING COOPERATIVE GAMES

Designing cooperative games is a fun and creative challenge. Once you know how, you can share your skills with your students, who will likely enjoy the process too.

How to Get Started

There is no right or wrong way to design games, but the following process works for me. The first thing to do is gather up all the information you have about your project. Are you working with a particular theme? For example, are you making a game to celebrate Valentine's Day? Or do you need to develop a game to teach algebra? Also, what materials can you use, how big is your group, and what skills, interests, abilities, and limitations do they have? Consider what types of cooperative games are suitable for your purpose. Perhaps you should develop a circle game or an active physical game or a board game? Or perhaps another format? It may help to write down all the relevant information you are starting with.

Next, brainstorm. If you possibly can find interested colleagues, collaborate here. Let ideas flow. Sketching helps. Think about other games you like. Do not copy any existing game mechanics. Rather, analyze how other games work and imagine how you can modify the mechanics in an original way to fit your purposes. If you are knowledgeable in cooperative learning activities, ponder those dynamics and see if you can gamify them. Games should be accessible to all. This involves keeping directions simple. At the same time, do not make your game too easy to win. Without challenge, games are boring. Also, losing can actually be fun in cooperative games, unlike competitive games. Losing together brings people together and motivates trying again. Matt Leacock (2013), designer of the runaway bestselling cooperative board game Pandemic, reportedly aims for players to win only about one-third of the time. Winning is fun too, of course! Learning to win together is the powerful, prosocial point of cooperative games, after all.

Think About Game Mechanics

As you begin to play cooperative games, you will become familiar with different kinds of game mechanics. This will be helpful for game design. Also, consider what Ruth Cornelius and Theo Lentz (1950), source of the earliest writing on cooperative games, had to say on the subject. They conceptualized five different kinds of cooperative game mechanics and gave examples of games they designed for each:

- *Simultaneous Finish:* The goal of the game is for all players to finish at the same time. For example, in Cooperative Checkers the two players try to get the black checkers and red checkers to the other side of the board at the same time.

- *Coordinated Manipulation:* All players try to coordinate their timing and execution with others so that objects are manipulated in a smooth pattern or rhythm. For example, in Cooperative Bowling, the goal of the game is to knock down the pins in as many rounds as there are players.
- *Rotation:* Each player takes a turn in sequence, so everyone is responsible for one step toward a progressive goal. For example, in Center Throw, players form a circle with one player standing in the center. The center player throws the ball to any player he chooses, then quickly runs to any player and takes his place. That player then runs to the center to catch the ball thrown by the last player receiving it. Play continues in this way around the circle.
- *Equal Division:* Players play so that the score or object of the game can be equally divided by the players at the end of the game. For example, a card game that ends when every player is holding cards that add up to a score of 20 demonstrates this principle.
- *Predetermined Score:* The object of the game is to reach a total score toward which all players have contributed. For example, in Cooperative Horseshoes, players decide in advance what score they will strive for and how many throws they will allow themselves to reach this score.

Quality Check: Features of Well-Designed Games

Once your game concept has taken shape, check it against Terry Orlick's (2006) four criteria for good cooperative games, which were mentioned earlier. If your game is deficient in any of the following aspects, revise it until your game is:

- Cooperative
- Inclusive
- Makes players feel accepted
- Fun

Designing for Cooperation

To design cooperation into your game, give every player a part to play. Use the concept of *positive interdependence*. That is, design the game so that all players perceive that their own success depends on everyone else in the group *and* that the group's success depends on their own contributions. How to do this? Use a division of labor where different players have the opportunity to share their particular, specialized talents, skills, or knowledge to help the group. Or simply make winning dependent on the participation of each player. Building discussion into the game and design features that require players to help one another or work together also build cooperation (Allen & Appelcline, 2018). For example, I designed a cooperative board game in 2017 with children's songwriter Raffi called The Baby Beluga Game. The game is won if Baby Beluga makes it all the way around the board. It is lost if players all lose their "heart cards" before Baby Beluga can complete his journey. If any single player loses all their heart cards during the game, other players who still have cards share so that no player is left "heartless" and alone. The card-sharing rule builds cooperation and sharing into the game.

Designing for Inclusivity

Designing inclusion into your game is important, too. All cooperative games are inclusive because no one can be eliminated and everyone is welcome to play. Beyond that basic rule, which is inherent to cooperative games, inclusivity depends on games being relatable and accessible to all your students.

Designing for Acceptance

How can you structure a game so that it makes players feel accepted? You might design it so that individual players are sure to receive positive attention. For example, in Clap Happy the entire group claps louder or softer to guide a player. It is an affirming experience to be in the midst of a group of people all frantically clapping for you! Also, games that require players to say each other's names impart feelings of acceptance. Games that reward expressiveness and spontaneity, such as Pass the Funny Face, help everyone feel seen, accepted, and enjoyed. Trust-building games, such as Trust Fall, let players feel vulnerable but then ultimately accepted and cared for.

Designing for Fun

Finally, our conversation turns to fun. Fun is that elusive element that turns mere activities into play. It is the delectable secret sauce that every cooperative game needs. How can you design fun into games? Creating fun is as much an art as a science, but there are principles to guide you. Some games are fun because they generate *cognitive delight*, as in the aha! experience that comes with solving puzzles. Other games are fun because they generate *intense emotional experiences*, such as curiosity, excitement, or amusement (Allen & Appelcline, 2018). This is why so many games that involve meeting a challenge are fun—they involve intense emotions of challenge as well as relief. Games that involve *humor* and *silliness* are often lots of fun. *Surprises* are fun, too. Games of chance are fun because dabbling with the factor of *luck* is intrinsically exciting and suspenseful. Games that *showcase players' personalities, talents, and skills* are also fun and entertaining because people-watching is fun. The excitement that comes with *performing* is fun as long as the group is supportive. *Sensory appeal*—for example, stunning graphics in a board game—enhances fun. *Sharing* and *helping* feel fun, too, though some students may not realize this at first. Prosocial behavior is ultimately fun in the sense that it elicits many pleasant feelings. These include emotions such as empathy, appreciation, compassion, and joy.

Time to Test Your Game

Test, identify problems, fix problems, and test again. Repeat with as many different groups as you can. The more you test, the better.

CONVERTING COMPETITIVE GAMES TO COOPERATIVE GAMES

Here are a few options for changing the mechanics of traditional competitive games to more cooperative versions.

- *Eliminate Scoring:* For example, in Ping-Pong, just play for the joy of it without bothering to keep score. Rally rather than compete.
- *Keep a Group Score, Rather Than Individual Scores:* In the Ping-Pong example, scoring could be based on consecutive hits. Challenge can be built into this if players focus on skill development. For example, they could agree to only count difficult shots returned in the overall score.
- *Make Scoring Contingent on Inclusion:* For example, in Up in the Air, the game can only be won if each group member taps a balloon suspended in the air.
- *Switch Team Members Often:* When playing team sports or games, have teams switch their members periodically throughout the game. This prevents us-versus-them thinking.
- *Equal Play Time for All:* Let all players play for the same amount of time. For example, every jumper in jump rope gets one full minute to jump regardless of how many times they need to restart.
- *Players Play All Positions:* In team sports, rotate players through all positions. For example, in softball, all players get to experience catching, pitching, and playing outfield. In volleyball, players simply rotate positions on each side of the net.

QUESTION FOR REFLECTION

3. Pick a competitive game that you have played. Now convert it to a cooperative version. Play it when you can. Then, after testing your game, revise it to make it better.

CHAPTER SUMMARY

Following five basic steps helps the teacher derive maximum educational value from a cooperative game. The first step is to choose a well-designed game that addresses the intended instructional goal. Then, carefully dealing with logistics, framing the game, leading it in an organized way, and leading postgame reflection are important steps. Teachers often need to adapt existing cooperative games to their particular teaching settings. Some like to design new games, too. Terry Orlick's four criteria of well-designed cooperative games can be used as a framework for this. Converting traditional competitive games to cooperative games is another way to generate new cooperative games. This can be done, for example, by keeping a group score rather than tallying players' scores separately.

PLAY TO LEARN—TRY THIS!

MOON BALL

This game works well for groups with as few as 6 to as many as 20 players. It requires one or more inflatable beach balls. It should be played in a large indoor or outdoor area.

Directions:

The goal of the game is for the group to keep the ball in the air for as many consecutive hits as possible (Figure 5.1). If the ball touches the ground, the count must start again from zero. No player can hit the ball more than once before another player hits it.

Framing

Ask the group how many times they think they will be able to hit the ball. Ask how this game is different than a competitive game. Ask players to discuss among themselves if they think this will be an easy or difficult task and

Figure 5.1. In Moon Ball, the group can only win when everyone participates.

why. Ask the players to figure out how they will be sure everyone taps the ball yet no one taps it consecutively.

Reflection

Ask players such questions as, "Did you achieve your goal? What were some of your challenges? How could the game be made to be more fun?"

Part III

APPLICATIONS OF COOPERATIVE GAMES

CHAPTER 6

Cooperative Games to Support Cooperative Learning

If humans are to learn to live cooperatively, they must experience the living process of cooperation in the schools.

—John Dewey

> In the pandemic, I have been helping my teenage kids with their online learning. We encountered the meme, posted many places online, that the people who were doing everything they're supposed to—staying home, socially distancing, wearing masks—were "the same people who did all the work in group projects." We nodded. This made us wonder, why are so many "cooperative" group projects at school unfair? When I was in school, it seemed like I always got stuck with all the work. People who didn't care about school just went along for the ride. Two of my kids are having that same problem with cooperative assignments now, but my third child has the opposite problem. He says that other students never listen to him or let him contribute. Cooperation is hard! Isn't there a way to make group projects more cooperative?
>
> —Jennifer, mother of three

Cooperative games and cooperative learning are closely linked. They are the two main approaches that educators use to teach cooperation. They both consist of cooperatively structured activities, so similar interpersonal dynamics underlie them both and explain their teaching power.

For all their similarities, cooperative learning and cooperative games have a basic difference. One is a method for doing work, while the other is a form of play. This difference makes them complementary. Cooperative games prepare students for cooperative learning by teaching them basic cooperative skills in a motivating and accessible way (Cohen, 1986). Using cooperative games to support cooperative learning is a winning strategy for teaching academic subjects, as this chapter will show.

BACKGROUND ON COOPERATIVE LEARNING

Brief History of Cooperative Learning

Cooperative learning is a philosophy of teaching as well as a collection of teaching methods. As discussed in Chapter 1, its roots are anchored in the writings of early 20th-century progressive education reformer John Dewey (Goldstein, 2002). Dewey (1916) argued that the public schools should teach students how to cooperate. He explained that teaching cooperation is essential to students' social development and to the sustainability of democratic society as well.

An early form of cooperative learning based on Dewey's views was widely implemented in the 1920s (Goldstein, 2002). However, it waned as America's competitive spirit intensified during the interwar period of the 1930s. In the 1940s, in the aftermath of World War II, the need for cooperation became abundantly clear once again. Social scientists, educators, and policy makers labored to better understand cooperation and develop ways to foster it. This time, the impetus was not the desire to safeguard democracy, but the quest for peace. Attempts to structure schoolwork cooperatively surfaced here and there in this context, though a cohesive theory and body of best practices was lacking. Then, in 1949, social psychologist Morton Deutsch put forth the theory that laid the foundation for a robust, modern model of cooperative learning. This was the theory of social interdependence, introduced in Chapter 2.

The basic tenet of social interdependence theory is that goal structure determines social interaction and social interaction determines the outcome of a situation. That is, when individuals share goals and work together toward them, the social effects are positive, and as a result the chances of attaining the goal are enhanced. Competition is the inverse proposition: when goal attainment is mutually exclusive, the social effects are negative, and as a result, the parties' prospects of achieving goals are hindered (Deutsch, 1949a).

The theory of social interdependence has had extraordinary impact beyond academia. Its principles are manifest in business practices that emphasize collaboration, in statecraft that facilitates win-win outcomes, in the field of peaceful conflict resolution, and in the schools where they are embodied as cooperative learning (Coleman, 2017).

QUESTION FOR REFLECTION

1. "The theory of social interdependence undercuts Social Darwinist notions that glorify competition as the prime mover of social progress. It also undercuts traditional ideals of rugged individualism that tell us heroes act alone." Do you agree with this statement? Why or why not?

The Modern Cooperative Learning Movement

The cooperative learning methods that are popular today are rooted in foundational work conducted in the late 1960s by David and Roger Johnson, professors of education at the University of Minnesota. David Johnson had been a student of Morton Deutsch at Columbia University. He learned the lessons of social interdependence well, for he and his brother Roger pioneered the application of them to education, as Morton Deutsch himself noted (Johnson & Johnson, 2011). The Johnsons thereby planted seeds for an approach to teaching that is now used widely all around the world.

Generally, cooperative learning consists of small groups of students working collaboratively on structured academic tasks. Students carry out their tasks without direct supervision by the teacher. Groups are heterogeneous with respect to ability level, learning style, gender, ethnicity, and other social factors. Group members are incentivized to help one another learn through various means, sometimes including the sharing of grades or other rewards (Goldstein, 2002).

Three of the most frequently used and thoroughly evaluated models of cooperative learning are:

- *Learning Together*, developed by the aforementioned Roger T. Johnson and David W. Johnson
- *Complex Instruction*, originated by Elizabeth Cohen of Stanford University
- *Student Teams—Achievement Divisions*, developed by Robert Slavin of Johns Hopkins University

These models and their methods have been validated and refined by hundreds of university studies as well as decades of classroom practice. While cooperative learning is not a panacea for all instructional problems, when conducted properly, it significantly enhances both academic achievement and social skills (Goldstein, 2002). Social interdependence theory would predict these results. "There is nothing as practical as a good theory," as Morton Deutsch's mentor Kurt Lewin once said (Johnson & Johnson, 2011, p. 60).

Cooperative group work addresses the systemic educational issue of inequity. When students with diverse abilities and backgrounds support one another's learning, problems of social dominance and unequal access to instruction diminish, and opportunities for everyone to learn multiply (Cohen & Lotan, 2014).

Cooperative Learning Task Design

However, implementing cooperative learning is not easy. It takes savvy instructional design and thorough preparation and planning. A cornerstone of good task design is inclusion of strategies that build *positive interdependence*. Positive interdependence is an earmark of true cooperation. It exists when all group members believe that group success depends on everyone doing their part, including themselves (Deutsch, 1949a). One way to embed positive interdependence is to make cooperative learning tasks complex in multifaceted ways. Such a task will not be easy for some and hard for others. This assures that group members realize they can get the job done faster, easier, and better if they work together. Similarly, structuring tasks to engage multiple abilities builds positive interdependence. If the skills and talents of all group members are needed, each student must depend on every other to complete the task. Distributing rewards among group members also helps to assure positive interdependence (Johnson & Johnson, 2011).

Different practitioners design cooperative learning in different ways, depending on their own priorities and the particulars of the teaching situation. Still, there is wide agreement that other features in addition to positive interdependence are important. One of them is *individual accountability*. This is a mechanism to be sure that each student is accountable for the contributions she makes. If a team member engages in "free-riding" or "social loafing"—letting other group members do all the work—he will be held responsible. Individual accountability can be achieved by grading students as individuals, by quizzing them separately, and in other ways.

Group processing is another common design feature among cooperative learning tasks. Group processing is a reflective discussion process in which group members talk about how well they are cooperating and achieving their goals and what they might do to improve. Group processing has been found to increase overall achievement among high-, medium-, and low-achieving students; to boost problem-solving; to enhance motivation; and to increase how much students encourage one another (Johnson & Johnson, 1989, 2005). Group processing also results in more friendships among differently abled students, improved self-esteem, and increased positive feelings about the subject area being studied (Johnson & Johnson, 2011).

But, regardless of how well-designed a cooperative learning task is, it cannot get off the ground if students have no capacity to collaborate. It is true that cooperative learning teaches cooperative behavior, but it does so by refining, reinforcing, and expanding on preexisting skills (Cohen & Lotan, 2014). Savvy cooperative learning practitioners prepare students to work together on academic tasks by teaching them basic cooperative skills in advance. So how exactly can teachers get the cooperative ball rolling? Perhaps, literally, by rolling a ball.

USING COOPERATIVE GAMES TO SUPPORT COOPERATIVE LEARNING

Cooperative games are an effective way to teach the social skills needed for cooperative learning, as Elizabeth Cohen explains in the first edition of *Designing Groupwork: Strategies for the Heterogeneous Classroom*:

The first step in introducing groupwork to a classroom is to prepare students for cooperative work situations. It is a great mistake to assume that children (or adults) know how to work with each other in a constructive collegial fashion . . . Students must be prepared for cooperation so that they know how to behave in the groupwork situation without direct supervision. It is necessary to introduce new cooperative behaviors in a training program. Preparing students for cooperative groups requires you to decide which norms and skills will be needed for the groupwork setting you have in mind. These norms and skills are best taught through exercises and *games* [emphasis added]. (1986, pp. 35–36)

Note that cooperative games are endorsed in this quote without explicitly naming the genre of "cooperative games." Cooperatively structured games are bundled with "activities" and "exercises" as the warm-ups or skill-builders needed for cooperation training. This is in keeping with the prevailing absence of recognition of cooperative games as a distinct pedagogical tool. If cooperative games were recognized for their uniqueness, their particular role in cooperation training could be tracked. Although Cohen's work does not compare the specific advantages of cooperative games to other exercises, it still clearly indicates that cooperative games are an effective tool for training students in cooperation prior to cooperative learning.

A COOPERATIVE GAMES TRAINING PROGRAM
FOR COOPERATIVE LEARNING

The following cooperative training program gives you the nuts-and-bolts of using cooperative games to prepare students for cooperative learning. It is my adaptation of cooperation training procedures described by Elizabeth Cohen and Rachel Lotan (2014), both of the Stanford Teacher Education Program (STEP), which I graduated from. I have made a few slight adjustments, for example, to give more information on finding games. The method is suitable for students of any age, kindergarten through grade 12.

Note that Cohen (with Lotan later) pioneered a version of cooperative learning called *complex instruction*. Complex instruction is like other models in its attention to positive interdependence, individual accountability, and social skills. However, it has a heightened focus on equity and the needs of heterogeneous classrooms. The training method offered here applies to cooperative learning in general and is not limited to complex instruction. Follow this routine before you launch a new cooperative learning activity:

1. Decide how your students will work together on the cooperative learning task you are training them for. What format will they use? Will the cooperative learning task involve group discussion? A learning center?

2. Decide on the games for cooperative training. What games will you use? Are there existing games you can adapt? Do you need to invent games?

3. Prep for your cooperative training program. Gather materials, check logistics, and anticipate needs.

4. It's cooperation training time! Let your students play a cooperative game—but use Bandura's (1969) *five principles of social learning* to maximize training value (given below). Also, don't forget to refer to the generic guidelines for facilitating cooperative games presented in Chapter 5.

5. Postgame discussion and debriefing is done for group processing. Lead the students in a discussion to reflect on their role in the game, the group's ability to cooperate in the game, and what to do differently next time.

6. Assess students' success before moving on to cooperative learning. Are students prepared sufficiently for the cooperative learning activity? Have they internalized norms and demonstrated sufficient cooperative skills? If so, begin. If not, play another cooperative game, or run an alternative cooperative activity or exercise.

We will now consider each of these steps of the training method in more granular terms.

Step 1: Identify the Cooperative Learning Task

Decide on the general nature of the cooperative learning task you will assign. Different groupwork tasks require different cooperative behaviors (Cohen & Lotan, 2014.) Your training program should teach the *same* cooperative behaviors as the cooperative learning task requires. Once you decide how students will need to work together on their academic task, you can identify the behaviors—that is, the social skills and norms—in which to train them. The learning task needn't be specified in great detail at this point. Two common cooperative learning task structures—*learning centers* and *discussion groups*—are listed in Table 6.1 along with the cooperative behaviors they require.

QUESTION FOR REFLECTION

2. If you are preparing students to work in a learning center format, name three behaviors that a training game should elicit.

Table 6.1. Student Behaviors Required in Learning Centers and Discussion Groups

Learning Centers	Discussion Groups
Asking questions	Asking for others' opinions
Listening	Listening
Helping others	Reflecting on what has been said
Helping students do things for themselves	Being concise
Showing others how to do things	Giving reasons for ideas
Explaining by telling how and why	Allowing everyone to contribute
Finding out what others think	Pulling ideas together
Making up your own mind	Finding out if group is ready to make a decision

(Cohen, 1986, p. 41; reprinted by permission of the publisher. From Elizabeth G. Cohen *Designing Groupwork: Strategies for the Heterogeneous Classroom*. Teachers College Press. Copyright ©1986 Elizabeth G. Cohen. All rights reserved.)

Step 2: Identify a Game to Teach a Specific Behavior

Now that you know what behaviors you want to activate, identify a game that will do so. You can either find a game or make one up. To find cooperative games, refer to books and websites (see Appendix B for suggestions). Some game manuals list the particular cooperative behaviors that the games teach. Do these match the behaviors you want to witness in your cooperative learning assignment? If you opt to create a game rather than adapt an existing one, refer to Chapter 5 of this book for tips on designing your own.

Be sure to select games that are easy enough for everyone to play. Choose games that pose an exciting challenge but have simple directions. There is no advantage in using games that are hard to learn how to play when you are teaching heterogeneous groups to cooperate. The goal is to immerse everyone in prosocial, inclusive fun as quickly and easily as you can.

Step 3: Do Your Prep

Be sure you understand game rules and have a plan for communicating them. You may wish to write the rules on a chalkboard or poster as well as read them aloud. Determine where the game will be played, and of course consider safety precautions such as the potential for tripping, falling, or bumping into one another. Be sure you have enough materials. Gather them up and arrange for volunteers to help you run the game as needed.

Step 4: Run the Game Using Bandura's Principles of Social Learning

Since you are using the game for training, teach skills and norms in a concerted, structured way. Use the principles of social learning that psychologist Albert Bandura (1969) developed through extensive experimentation. Bandura's principles of social learning are simple, practical, and effective in a wide range of settings where new behaviors are being taught to children or adults. They are summarized by Cohen and Lotan (2014) as follows:

1. New behaviors are labeled and discussed.
2. Students learn to recognize when new behaviors occur.
3. Students are able to use labels and discuss behaviors in an objective way.
4. Students have a chance to practice new behaviors.
5. New behaviors are reinforced when they occur. (pp. 49–50)

You have a good chance of observing the cooperative behaviors you want as long as you implement these five principles. Let us look carefully at how to apply them with a specific example.

Suppose, for example, that you are training students for later work at a learning center. You have identified the cooperative behavior "helping students do things for themselves" as one that you want to teach. You have also identified a game that prompts students to use this behavior. Your training game involves students standing in a large circle outside and tossing a Frisbee to one another. The group wins when the Frisbee gets passed from student to student all the way around the circle without hitting the ground. Because every student needs to be able to catch and throw the Frisbee, the game rules motivate students to want to help one another. Now that you have done the first three steps outlined in the cooperative training program, you are ready for the fourth step, running the game.

QUESTION FOR REFLECTION

3. Which step of the cooperative training method involves using Bandura's principles of social learning?

Let the game begin. Explain to the students that they will be playing a cooperative game to prepare themselves for working together on an academic task. Explain that the game will give them practice in the same cooperative behavior they will need to use on their academic task. Discuss the behavior "helping students do things for themselves." As you do this, you are fulfilling social learning principle number 1, labeling and discussing the new behavior.

When students play the game, they are practicing new behavior (social principle number 4 on the list above). Good. You can also satisfy principle number 2 (recognizing new behaviors) and principle number 3 (using labels and discussing behavior) during gameplay with the following strategy:

> Appoint one student to act as the group Observer while the others play.
> The Observer counts every time he sees (recognizes) group members displaying the behavior "helping students do things for themselves."
> At the end of the game, the Observer tells the players how many times they exhibited the behavior and what the behavior looked like.

You have the chance to fulfill the fifth principle of social learning—reinforcing a new behavior as it occurs—if Observers report what happens in their groups while students play.

Step 5: Postgame Reflection

When the game is over and students have played as many rounds as needed, you have reached the fifth step in the training method. Foster discussion to help students reflect on their individual and group experience. Ask questions about how they demonstrated the cooperative behavior the game focused on, such as specifically how and when they did it and how it contributed to their own success as well as the group's. Also ask the group to discuss among themselves how they could have cooperated more fully. Knowing that behavior involves both *norms* and *skills,* help students become aware of the norms they followed (for example, letting everyone participate equally or responding to the needs of the group) and the skills they practiced (for example, listening closely and asking for assistance). When they have developed these insights, point out how the cooperation they experienced corresponds to the cooperative behavior needed in the planned group work. As you facilitate self-reflection and group processing, avoid a lecturing tone. Be a "guide on the side," not a "sage on the stage."

Step 6. Assess Success

Before moving on to the cooperative learning activity, evaluate whether students can cooperate. Have they internalized the norm of fair and respectful cooperation? Have they demonstrated competency in cooperative skills? If they have, move on to cooperative learning. If not, play another cooperative game. Repeat the process until the students have learned cooperative skills and are motivated to use them. They will need these skills to work well together in academic cooperative learning.

CHAPTER SUMMARY

Cooperative learning consists of students working together in small groups and in a structured way to accomplish academic tasks. In order for cooperative learning to be successful, students must be able to cooperate. It cannot be assumed that all students understand how to behave cooperatively, however. Therefore, experts advise teachers to prepare their students for cooperative learning with activities that teach basic cooperative skills and motivation. Cooperative games, of course, do this. They are therefore quite helpful as a stepladder, helping all students access the high levels of achievement and social development that cooperative learning can take them to.

Cooperative games are a highly versatile teaching tool. In the next chapter, you will see that they are not only a powerful aid to cooperative learning, they are also a natural for teaching the "soft skills."

PLAY TO LEARN—TRY THIS!

TWO TRUTHS AND A LIE

This game can be used as preparation for discussion-based cooperative learning tasks. For help isolating cooperative behaviors associated with discussion groups, you can refer to Table 6.1. Two Truths and a Lie works well for groups of 4 to 6 students and is appropriate for middle and high school students. It takes about 30 minutes to play.

Directions:

Ask students to write three statements about themselves on a piece of paper (Figure 6.1). Two statements should be true while the third is a lie. In addition, the students should represent each statement with a simple drawing, through pantomime, with a song, or by another creative expression. There is a time limit of 10 minutes on this part of the game. Students next take turns presenting their statements and creative representations to one another. Group members try to detect the lie by asking two questions each. Afterward, they discuss and vote on a final decision as to which statement was false.

Figure 6.1. Two Truths and a Lie is a fun verbal cooperative game that promotes communication and connection.

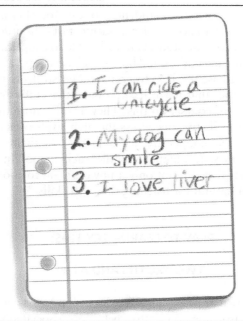

CHAPTER 7

Cooperative Games and the "Soft Skills"

Creating a space that is safe enough to feel as if one belongs requires more than just the intention to do so. . . . It requires a set of actions, behaviors, and attitudes that support those intentions. It means creating a space that people will not just feel invited into but connected to and can fully participate in.

—Larry Yang, *Author of Awakening Together* (2017)

Emily is a 3rd-grade teacher who uses cooperative board games to create a classroom climate where kindness and cooperation are the norm. In this recorded dialogue, Emily shows how to use postgame reflection to reinforce the lessons of the games:

Emily: What was the object of the game you just played, Luca?

Luca: Mainly the object was to get all the way to Granny's house and not get lost in the forest, or get taken away by the river, or eaten by a bear and stuff like that.

Emily: Tony, what did you learn about working with your teammates in this game?

Tony: I learned that if you have possessions of your own, you can use them to help other people. Like by giving honey to the bear, you can save your entire team from going all the way back!

Emily: Noah, what do you think would happen if you guys didn't all work together?

Noah: If we didn't work together, everyone will (*sic*) probably just be against each other and we will probably just keep losing the game.

TEACHING THE WHOLE STUDENT

Change is coming. There is a movement under way in American education to embrace the whole student—left brain, right brain, head, heart, and hand. Schools have traditionally concentrated on the cognitive domain with laserlike focus. Increasingly, though, schools recognize that it is important to teach the "soft skills." These are the skills and dispositions needed for happy and stable relationships, for emotional regulation and behavioral self-management, for self-awareness and self-care, and for treating each other with care.

The motivation for this movement is multifold. In part, it stems from discoveries in the learning sciences showing that the social and emotional faculties are deeply entwined with the cognitive domain (Jones & Kahn, 2017). Another driver is concern about the psychological stresses that students face today. Children impacted by trauma, poverty, racism, social division, and rampant stress related to media, hectic lifestyles, environmental hazards, the COVID pandemic, and so forth benefit from interventions that protect mental health (Pawlo, Lorenzo, Eichert, & Ellis, 2019.) Also, since social skills underlie success in the workplace, there is an argument for teaching social, emotional, and character development for career readiness. Humanists regard student well-being as an appropriate educational goal in and of itself. And in the end, it is clear that the health of a democratic society depends on the overall health and well-being of its citizenry, as John Dewey (1916) proclaimed. Truly, there are many reasons for moving beyond the narrowly defined cognitive domain to embrace the whole student!

Given the mission of teaching soft skills, educators must address the question of how to do it. Effective tools and methods are needed. Cooperative games are a very practical, versatile, and effective option, as I shall endeavor to show in this chapter. The discussion is organized in terms of three different though related conceptual models that foster whole-student education: *social-emotional learning (SEL); classroom climate*; and *moral education*. I begin by relating cooperative games to social-emotional learning—a curriculum reform movement with very strong momentum.

PEDAGOGY OF COOPERATIVE GAMES FOR SOCIAL AND EMOTIONAL LEARNING

Theoretical Rationale for Cooperative Games in SEL

Social-emotional learning is "the process through which we learn to recognize and manage emotions, care about others, make good decisions, behave ethically and responsibly, develop positive relationships, and avoid negative behaviors," according to Maurice Elias, director of Rutgers University's Social and Emotional Learning Lab (Edutopia, 2011). Would you predict that cooperative games can help students achieve the broad aims of SEL? Check yourself by answering the question below.

QUESTION FOR REFLECTION

1. Is there a social-psychological theory of cooperation and competition that would predict that cooperative games can attain the educational goals of SEL? If so, name the theory and explain how it works.

You learned about the *theory of social interdependence* in Chapters 2 and 6. It is the seminal social-psychological theory developed by Morton Deutsch in 1949 that documents the disparate social effects of cooperation versus competition. People interact differently, displaying an entirely different set of attitudes and behaviors, when they share a goal and work together versus when they work against one another. Where there is cooperation, prosocial behavior flourishes (Johnson & Johnson, 2011).

Because well-designed cooperative games are structured to provide a meaningful experience of cooperation, students experience the good feelings and social rewards that come with cooperation, including caring, respect, and kinship. They discover for themselves that "it's nice to be nice." Cooperative games teach social-emotional awareness through personal discovery. This involves students' faculties all working together—head, heart, and hand. This is quite a different way to learn SEL concepts, skills, and values compared to direct instruction.

Research Supporting Cooperative Games for SEL

From a theoretical standpoint, then, one would expect that cooperative games would be a powerful way to teach SEL. Is there also evidence to support this? Yes, happily, there is. As introduced in Chapter 2, the research conducted by cooperative games pioneer Terry Orlick (1983) points to the social and emotional effects of cooperative games:

> One major goal of cooperative learning experiences is to enable children of the future to become more receptive to sharing both human and material resources (e.g., ideas, talents, concerns, feelings, respect, possessions, equipment, turns, time, space, responsibility, and the betterment of each other's lives). With this in mind, a series of games was created, and several studies were conducted to assess the social impact of well-designed cooperative game programs. The results have consistently shown an increase in cooperative behavior in games, in free play, and in the classroom setting for children involved in these programs. The cooperative change does not occur overnight, but over a period of several months, most children seem to become more considerate and caring human beings. (p. 156)

Arnold Goldstein, also discussed in Chapter 2, conducted similar studies. His experiments included young adults and teenagers as well as young children. In 2002, Goldstein summarized his findings: "In all, cooperative gaming, much like cooperative learning, has been shown to yield reliable and substantial cooperation-enhancing and related prosocial effects in both elementary and secondary level students" (p. 148).

Other researchers including Bay-Hinitz et al. have also concluded that children learn skills for prosocial interaction through playing cooperative games (1994). Thus there is research and theory supporting the ever-so-intuitive claim that cooperative games are a viable instrument for conducting SEL.

Cooperative Games and Current SEL Frameworks

In recent years, SEL has become a robust and organized educational reform movement. To a large extent it is spearheaded by the Collaborative for Academic, Social, and Emotional Learning (CASEL). Along with many state-level educational framework committees and various other research and policy organizations, CASEL (2020a) has been developing SEL standards and guidelines for best practice for over a decade. These standards, guidelines, and frameworks determine what SEL methods are adopted by the schools. Fortunately, cooperative games can be correlated to these documents in very specific ways, providing a formal and up-to-date rationale for the practice.

The CASEL framework breaks SEL down into five core competencies: *self-awareness, social awareness, responsible decision-making, self-management,* and *relationship skills.* The five competencies can be taught at all developmental stages from childhood to adulthood and in diverse cultural contexts (CASEL, 2020b). Of the five competencies, *relationship skills* is the one that most obviously aligns closely with cooperative games. As you read this portion of the CASEL framework below, notice how squarely cooperative games target this core competency.

> RELATIONSHIP SKILLS: The abilities to establish and maintain healthy and supportive relationships and to effectively navigate settings with diverse individuals and groups. This includes the capacities to communicate clearly, listen actively, cooperate, work collaboratively to problem-solve and negotiate conflict constructively, navigate settings with differing social and cultural demands and opportunities, provide leadership, and seek or offer help when needed, such as:
> * Communicating effectively
> * Developing positive relationships
> * Demonstrating cultural competency
> * Practicing teamwork and collaborative problem-solving
> * Resolving conflicts constructively
> * Resisting negative social pressure
> * Showing leadership in groups

- Seeking or offering support and help when needed
- Standing up for the rights of others

We will correlate cooperative games to just one of the elements on this list as an example. Consider the first one, communicating effectively. Do cooperative games teach this skill? Certainly they do. Cooperative games are all about working together to reach a goal. Working together well requires excellent communication. To win a strategy-based cooperative game, for example, players coordinate their actions through group planning and decision-making. Explaining, listening, negotiating, compromising, nonverbal communication, and more are typical parts of the process. So, absolutely, cooperative games give students practice in constructive communication. Check! Can you see how fulsomely cooperative games fulfill all the other elements of the relationship skills competency?

Choices for SEL Implementation

Knowing that cooperative games have a solid basis in theory and research and that they are consistent with contemporary SEL practice, the next issue is nuts-and-bolts implementation. What might the practice of cooperative games toward SEL look like?

You might want to simply put cooperative games in your toolkit (refer to Chapter 4) and pull them out whenever you have a little extra time. When the class finishes an assignment early, for instance, you could run a game that works for your entire class. Or, on a rainy day when recess is cancelled, you could run several games at the same time in gallery format. In this case the games are separate and freestanding, and students play them in series. Be sure to consider carefully the games you use for their social and emotional learning value. For example, consider which of the CASEL relationship skills a given game teaches.

You can use cooperative games for SEL in a more concerted way by conducting the cooperation training program described in Chapter 6. This program teaches cooperation and other social skills, so it has value as an SEL method whether or not it is used as a precursor to cooperative learning. The training program is based on principles of social learning and cooperative learning that are verified by decades of strong research and scholarship (Bandura, 1969; Cohen, 1986).

Another approach is to integrate cooperative games across the curriculum and thereby incorporate SEL into much of what students do each day. You can insert them into the school day on a regular basis in a variety of ways. For example, use them during circle time, as a recess activity, and to teach subject-area content. The integrative approach is aligned with current best-practice guidelines. According to the Aspen Institute, an educational policy organization:

Integration is essential . . . When academic, social, and emotional components are effectively woven into the fabric of a school, students develop skills to manage and take care of themselves; to get along and work well within their learning communities; to successfully engage in academic learning; and to serve as responsible and participating members of their communities. (Edwards, 2017, p. 4)

Last but not least, you can use cooperative games as an SEL "signature practice." CASEL published a handy guide called *SEL 3 Signature Practices Playbook, A Tool That Supports Systemic SEL* (2019). The *Playbook* distills CASEL's voluminous recommendations down to just three that make SEL easily doable for everyone right away. It is easy to see that cooperative games embody the first signature practice, "welcoming/inclusion activities." Cooperative games are inclusive by their very definition because no one is eliminated, and everyone has a part to play. The fun factor is icing on the cake for inclusion, since social divisions and self-consciousness melt when people have fun together. Chapter 4 lists several cooperative games that you can use to welcome all learners to class and start the day off on a positive note. Chapter 5 tells you how to make your own games for welcoming and inclusion. It also provides other tips for facilitating cooperative games to maximize their SEL value.

COOPERATIVE GAMES AND CLASSROOM CLIMATE

The Meaning of Classroom Climate

Have you ever found yourself in a classroom where you didn't feel safe? Where you felt like you didn't belong? Like the teacher and your classmates didn't see, appreciate, or approve of who you are? In such a social environment, would you feel confident enough to ask questions? Would you arrive on time, sit eagerly toward the front of the room, make eye contact with others? Or would you stay toward the back, lower your eyes, try your best not to be seen, and psychologically distance yourself? Might you be disruptive or rebel to protect yourself in a different way?

It is *classroom climate*, the social-psychological classroom milieu, that determines whether or not you feel safe in school. If the climate is not inclusive, if you feel rejected or that you do not belong, if the environment is perceived to be full of psychological threat, the classroom is an alienating place where you will suffer. On the other hand, when classroom climate is positive, being there is a pleasure. You enjoy working with other students as well as on your own. Learning, growing, playing, and exploring are a happy adventure when you have a sense of purpose, joy, and belonging, and a beloved teacher guiding the way.

SEL practices can help build a positive classroom climate, but SEL and classroom climate are not the same thing. SEL is a curriculum reform movement. The climate of a classroom or school, on the other hand, is ambient, diffuse, something you feel. It is all about mood and tone. It is the sum total of myriad interactions among students and teachers as well as subtle cues about what and who is welcome. Teachers can do much to influence classroom climate. However, it is a co-creation that expresses the attitudes and feelings of each person in the room. Peer-to-peer interactions are a major contributor. Classroom climate reflects the classroom's culture.

Besides teacher-student and peer-to-peer interactions, other factors contribute to classroom climate. These include the physical environment—whether the room is aesthetically pleasing; representative of students' cultures, tastes, genders, and identities; of comfortable temperature; well-lit with comfortable places to sit; free of overstimulating, sexist, racist, ableist, or culturally insensitive decor; accommodating of physical needs.

Using Cooperative Games to Create a Positive Classroom Climate

Play can uplift classroom climate by spreading joy and mirth. Cooperative games, being a form of play, have this capacity. It is highly debatable whether competitive games also improve classroom climate by bringing joyful play to bear. Remember from Chapter 1 that outcome does not matter in play, by definition. A truly playful activity is nonthreatening and worry-free. Yet in competitive games, outcome often does matter in a serious way because the scathing label of "loser" hangs in the air as a psychological threat. There is no such threat with cooperative games. Play is indeed carefree, devoid of threat, and promotive of feeling safe. It is a pure joy that helps make the classroom climate a positive one.

A school or classroom's climate can only feel safe and nurturing if *everyone* feels included. Inclusivity is an obvious attribute of cooperative games, as emphasized throughout this book. When the teacher selects cooperative games as a classroom activity, she signals her embrace of inclusivity as a norm. Her care and concern for each and every one of her students is expressed. Students absorb the message that everyone is welcome and safe. No one needs to fear exclusion or rejection for not being "good enough." Everyone gets to play!

Classroom climate, of course, depends enormously on how students treat one another. From the child's perspective, when mean or aggressive peers lurk in the room, there is no telling when they might fling some nastiness your way. The environment cannot feel fully relationally safe when peer-to-peer meanness, domination, and aggression are afoot. Here again, cooperative games provide a strategic solution. As has been said previously in this chapter and elsewhere in this book, studies have shown cooperative games increase prosocial behavior and decrease aggression both during and after the game (Bay-Hinitz et al., 1994; Goldstein, 2002). These results accord with the theory of social interdependence, which demonstrates that cooperation tends to produce prosocial behavior, while competition promotes hostility and aggression.

Cooperative games have been enjoyed for decades and have a cult following of enthusiasts who use them to build community, foster healthy relationships, and promote peace. Thus, when the teacher's objective is to foster a positive classroom climate by preventing antisocial behavior, she is well-advised to reach into her bag of teaching strategies and pull out a cooperative game.

QUESTION FOR REFLECTION

2. Name at least three ways that cooperative games reduce psychological threat in a classroom.

COOPERATIVE GAMES FOR MORAL EDUCATION

Moral Education and Public Education

Moral education is a deeper and more controversial endeavor than teaching SEL or trying to cultivate a positive classroom climate. Moral education aims to prepare the student for the moral ambiguities of real life. What should I do in this particular situation? What is the *right* thing to do? Moral education helps students build the inner resources needed to grapple with thorny moral dilemmas and, in the end, make choices defensible to their own conscience.

Moral education quickly becomes problematic in the public schools. There are no absolute and universal standards of "good" and "evil" or "right" and "wrong" to teach as one might teach the letters of the alphabet or the theorems of geometry. Morality is personal, developmental, debatable, and contextual. Notions of morality can be politically charged. In a pluralistic society founded on religious freedom, there are well-founded concerns that teaching specific moral values in public schools would infringe on religious freedom. And yet there is a need, today as always, for youth to receive support, guidance, and inspiration as they develop their moral beliefs and personal conscience.

Caring Theory and Cooperative Games

Cooperative games offer a way to conduct moral education that does not tread on religious freedom or personal autonomy because it is not based on the teaching of specific moral values. The crux of the approach is to use cooperative games to help students develop the ability to care for one another, and to understand the value and importance of caring feelings.

This perspective on moral education is grounded in a theory of moral development called *caring theory*, which was conceived in the 1980s by Stanford professor of educational philosophy Nel Noddings. It is described in her book *Caring: A Feminine Approach to Ethics and Moral Education* (1984). In this theory, the wellspring of moral behavior is located in caring relations, rather than in intellectual concepts that define good and evil. That is, Noddings argues that moral behavior grows out of the feeling of caring, rather than the desire to align with values prescribed by a moral code. So moral education consists of nurturing the student's ability to care rather than defining what is good versus bad. It is a heart-based approach, you might say. Teaching practices that encourage caring are the foundation of moral education in this view.

As has been mentioned many times in this book, cooperative games have been shown to increase behaviors that can be inferred to reflect an attitude of caring. These behaviors include helping others, encouraging, sharing, and showing signs of affection (Bay-Hinitz et al., 1994; Goldstein, 2002; Orlick, 1983). To the extent that cooperative games are able to foster feelings of caring and reinforce norms of caring, they help students develop a caring attitude.

Given an attitude of caring that is strengthened if not rooted in the joyous experience of cooperative play, students are ready to apply, practice, and deepen their caring feelings through moral action. The teacher can help students do this by employing a variety of teaching strategies. He might, for example, ask students to identify their caring feelings in a postgame debriefing. In combination with this, students might engage in service projects such as caring for animals or plants, teaching younger students, or giving holiday cards to seniors in community care homes.

QUESTION FOR REFLECTION

3. The potential of cooperative games to teach moral behavior lies in the experience of caring that good games elicit. Describe a cooperative game that could elicit caring.

CHAPTER SUMMARY

No longer confined strictly to the cognitive realm, teachers are increasingly addressing the social, emotional, and even the moral development of their students. Social-emotional learning (SEL) is now a common part of the curriculum. Cooperative games align with many approaches to SEL, including the influential CASEL framework, where the games clearly align with the relationship skills core competency. Cooperative games also can be used as a practice for welcoming and inclusion, which makes them a "signature practice"—in other words, a teaching strategy that should be used often, according to CASEL. Classroom climate, the overall feeling and milieu of the classroom, can be improved with cooperative games, too. They are a vehicle for joy through play; they are inclusive, so they promote a sense of belonging; and they help reduce peer-to-peer aggression, which improves students' sense of safety in the classroom. Finally, cooperative games can be applied to the task of moral education. The games have been shown to increase children's expressions of caring for one another. This is important because, according to Nel Noddings's caring theory of moral education, caring is the fundamental human experience upon which moral development is based.

This chapter has focused on using cooperative games to promote prosocial behavior. The following chapter looks at the other side of the coin—using cooperative games to prevent aggressive behavior. As you will see, playing together peacefully can be used to disrupt the social dynamics that give rise to interpersonal violence.

PLAY TO LEARN—TRY THIS!

TRUST FALL

This game works well best for students age 10 and up. A group of approximately 6 to 12 players stands in a circle, shoulder-to-shoulder. A volunteer stands in the middle. When everyone is ready, the volunteer falls with arms at his side and feet in place into the surrounding ring of friends. Needless to say, this builds trust. Take commonsense precautions with this game: Play it on a soft surface. It can take quite a bit of strength to support a volunteer who really trusts and lets go, so please be sure your group is up to the task!

Figure 7.1. Trust Fall is a classic cooperative game that, for obvious reasons, builds trust.

CHAPTER 8

Cooperative Games to Prevent Aggression

No one is born hating another person because of the color of his skin or his background or his religion. People must learn to hate, and if they can learn to hate, they can be taught to love. For love comes more naturally to the human heart than its opposite.

—Nelson Mandela

Arthur was . . . insecure at home and starved for love and affection. He had been in the habit of throwing temper tantrums. Sometimes when he came in from recess after a competitive game of marbles, he was red in the face, almost bursting from anger, knocking at anything and everything in his way. When he played a cooperative game however, his control was never taxed to the same degree. Losing a cooperative game seemed to be made bearable by the fact that others shared the loss with him, and that he had not been vanquished by another team.

—Ruth Cornelius & Theo Lentz, 1950

Hostility and aggression, at varying levels of intensity, are endemic to the world we live in. Why is cruelty an everyday fact of life when people are so capable of love, caring, and cooperation? What can the teacher do to reduce antisocial behavior at school so the "better angels" hold sway in the classroom? How can cooperative games help? These are the concerns of this chapter.

THE AGGRESSIVE STUDENT

Aggression is "behavior that results in personal injury and physical destruction. The injury may be physical, or it may involve psychological impairment through disparagement and abusive use of coercive power" (Bandura, 1983, p. 2). Aggression can be perpetrated by individuals as well as by groups.

Individual Aggression

There are numerous conditions that give rise to student aggression. Individuals may act aggressively due to *biological* factors such as hormonal imbalances (Ramirez, 2003). *Situational* factors such as the anonymity of an online chat room (Weingartner & Stahel, 2019) can encourage lone actors to express aggressive feelings as well. Some people are taught to act aggressively by family, friends, media figures, and others who model the behavior. This is the process of *social learning* described by Bandura (1983).

Competition is another factor that can cause aggression in individuals. Morton Deutsch (1985), developer of social interdependence theory, described the social effects of competition on individuals this way:

> In a competitive relationship, one is predisposed to cathect the other negatively, to have a suspicious, hostile, exploitive attitude toward the other, to be psychologically closed to the other, to be aggressive and defensive toward the other, to seek advantage and superiority for self and disadvantage and inferiority for the other, to see the other as opposed to oneself and basically different, and so on. One is also predisposed to expect the other to have the same orientation. (p. 85)

Given the extent of competition in school, it is really no surprise that some students act out aggressively. Educator Joseph Wax describes the situation forcefully (if a bit insultingly to us teachers):

> One must marvel at the intellectual quality of a teacher who can't understand why children assault one another in the hallway, playground and city street, when in the classroom the highest accolades are reserved for those who have beaten their peers. In many subtle and not so subtle ways, teachers demonstrate that what children learn means less than that they triumph over their classmates. Is this not assault? . . . Classroom defeat is only the pebble that creates widening circles of hostility. It is self-perpetuating. It is reinforced by peer censure, parental disapproval, and loss of self-concept. If the classroom is a model, and if that classroom models competition, assault in the hallways should surprise no one. (as cited in Kohn, 1986, p. 147)

Using Cooperative Games to Reduce Aggression in Individuals

When cooperative games are played in school, they help replace norms of competition with norms of cooperation. Norms of cooperation send the message that winning by beating others is not the goal. Prosocial behavior is expected—and celebrated. Students who act aggressively because they regard school as a competitive battleground can begin to heal by seeing they do not have to be "better than" to be "good enough."

Moreover, cooperative games can decrease aggression among individuals who display chronic prosocial deficiencies in school. Arnold Goldstein pioneered this approach, and it is fully described in his book *The Prepare Curriculum: Teaching Prosocial Competencies* (1999). As Goldstein explains, some aggressive youth act out because they literally do not know how to get along peacefully with others. When this is the case, increasing sociability is a matter of *replacing* learned antisocial behaviors with learned prosocial behaviors (Goldstein, 2002). Cooperative games teach cooperative skills and other prosocial behaviors and so are an effective tool in this regard.

Cooperative games are not just used to decrease aggression among aggressive individuals in school. Psychotherapists also use cooperative games as an intervention in therapeutic settings to decrease angry and aggressive behavior in young patients, as reported by Bay-Hinitz (2001).

GROUP AGGRESSION: FIGHTING TOGETHER

We now turn to the subject of group aggression. *Group aggression* is simply aggression conducted among groups of people. That is, one or more groups are the perpetrators, and one or more groups are the targets (Goldstein, 2002). Common forms are ostracism; bullying; feuding; hatemongering, rumor-spreading; trolling, doxing, and making threats online; riots; rebellions; gang violence; mob violence; war; and genocide. As Goldstein stated, "Human history, written with a gloomy but accurate pen, is a litany of groups of persons seeking to hurt other such groups" (Preface). We know from social interdependence theory that competition is implicated as a factor in antisocial behavior, but is it just one of many? Can we dig a little deeper? Is there a unifying theory of group aggression, that is, a framework for understanding why indeed human history is a litany of groups trying to hurt one another? We are looking for the systemic forces that underlie our eternal plight.

Realistic Conflict Theory: Competition as the Root of Group Aggression

Social psychologists are among the many to have pondered the origins of intergroup violence. Astoundingly, perhaps, since competition rides with us like a familiar passenger in the family car, competition is once again implicated as causing violence. Goldstein gets right to the point in Chapter 1 of his classic text, *The Psychology of Group Aggression* (2002), when he identifies competition as the ultimate culprit. He says:

> Competition between groups in the real world—nations, tribes, athletic teams, gangs, ethnic groups, and others—is a pervasive and enduring phenomenon, a phenomenon of major social and political salience and significance. As Forsyth (1983) observes: "The simple hypothesis that conflict is caused by competition

over valued but scarce resources has been used to explain the origin of class struggles (Marx & Engels, 1947), rebellions (Gurr, 1970), international warfare (Struefert & Streufert, 1979), and the development of culture and social structures (Simmel, 1950, p. 377; Sumner, 1906, p. 4).

This is a sweeping statement, and a startling indictment of a widely accepted norm. Yet, though the claim may seem grand, the central role of competition in group aggression is a bedrock principle of social psychology. The idea was originally put forth by social psychologist Muzafer Sherif (1958). Today, in its elaborated form, it is known as *realistic conflict theory,* or RCT.

RCT differs from social interdependence theory in its specific focus on the causal role of competition in group aggression. Social interdependence theory is broader in its examination of competition and cooperation. It investigates social effects as well as the impact of competition on goal achievement. Also, while social interdependence theory establishes that cooperation and competition have divergent social effects, it does not delve very deeply into the psychological processes that occur in the minds of the participants. By contrast, realistic conflict theory explores the cognitive processes and group dynamics that are intertwined with competition.

RCT posits intergroup competition as a zero-sum interaction between social groups such that rewards can only be achieved by one side. The rewards may be material goods such as food, wealth, territory, jobs, and so on. Or they may be intangible social goods such as power or fame. In any case, one group's win comes at the expense of another's loss. In this sense, conflict among competing groups is "realistic." It is based on actual prizes that can be won or lost. And so there is a rational basis for competing groups to view one another as threats, and this is exactly what they do (Goldstein, 2002).

Lamentably, the perception of group threat birthed by competition triggers exaggerated, fight-or-flight emotions (Kohn, 1986), suppresses empathy (Weingartner & Stahel, 2019), and sets up an "us-against-them" group dynamic that is anything but objectively grounded (Goldstein, 2002). Us-versus-them thinking cannot be the basis of calm and fair coexistence because it involves false and distorted perceptions of in-group and out-group members (Goldstein, 2002). Exaggerated positive qualities are attributed to the in-group ("in-group favoritism"), while the out-group gets painted with negative qualities, shortcomings, and failings well beyond what may be true ("out-group discrimination"). This intergroup bias arising from competition plants the seeds of chauvinism, prejudice, and quite possibly (depending on the particulars of the groups and setting) hostility and outright group aggression. As social psychologists Sidanius and Pratto (1999) describe:

> The perception that one group's gain is another's loss [from competition] translates into perceptions of group threat, which in turn cause prejudice against the outgroup, negative stereotyping of the outgroup, ingroup solidarity, [heightened]

awareness of intergroup identity, and internal cohesion including intolerance of ingroup deviants, ethnocentrism, use of boundary markers and discriminatory behavior. (p. 17)

A Classic Experiment: Robber's Cave

The Robber's Cave Experiment and other studies by Sherif provide a snapshot of the escalation process. In a 1961 study, a couple dozen boys attended a simulated summer camp for three weeks. Though the camp appeared to be typical in every way, with plenty of swimming, boating, and hiking, it was actually staffed by social science researchers disguised as counselors. Upon their arrival at camp, the boys were settled into two widely separated locations so they would have no contact with one another. During the first week, they formed friendships and established a group structure with norms and roles. Each group chose a name—one became the *Rattlers* and the other the *Eagles*. The groups were *cohesive*, meaning that there was a strong sense of unity and solidarity within them and a willingness to support the group's actions (Goldstein, 2002).

Toward the end of the first week, the boys learned that they were not alone. In fact, they were sharing the camp facilities with another group. Though the Rattlers and Eagles had not met, the groups began referring to each other as "those guys" in rivalrous terms. Soon, both groups began begging their "counselors" for opportunities to meet and compete in zero-sum encounters such as tent-pitching contests. The "counselors" (actually researchers) complied, all the while documenting an increasingly adversarial climate (Goldstein, 2002). A rapid escalation from sporting competition to overt hostility was observed, as is described below:

> At first, the tension between the two groups was limited to verbal insults, name calling, and teasing. Soon, however, the intergroup conflict escalated into full-fledged hostilities. After losing a bitterly contested tug-of-war battle, the Eagles sought revenge by taking down a Rattler flag and burning it . . . A fist fight [followed]. Next, raiding began, as the Rattlers sought revenge by attacking the Eagles' cabin tearing out the mosquito netting, overturning beds, and carrying off personal belongings. During this period, the attitudes of each group toward the other became more negative, but the cohesiveness of each [group] became stronger. (Forsyth, 1983, pp. 375–376)

QUESTION FOR REFLECTION

1. Why does intergroup competition lead to the perception of group threat, and why is this a problem?

Social Identity Theory: My Group Is Better Than Yours

Realistic conflict theory greatly advanced understanding of group aggression by identifying the us-versus-them group dynamics at its root. However, RCT did not answer every important question. Subsequent researchers have revised the early theory to better account for various empirical findings. For example, as it turns out, competition over real resources is a *sufficient* condition for intergroup hostility, but not a *necessary* one. In fact, groups do not need to compete over actual prizes to engage in us-versus-them thinking. As shown in laboratory experiments, groups that have had no social contact, know next to nothing about one another, and ostensibly are not competing over anything still develop such an attitude (Goldstein, 2002). Mere awareness of the presence of an out-group is enough to launch in-group favoritism and out-group discrimination and the associated adversarial group dynamics. Recall that the Rattlers and the Eagles expressed intergroup rivalry without ever having met. RCT did not explain the hostility that germinated before the groups had anything to compete over.

Social identity theory, developed by Henri Tajfel in the 1960s, explains that there is a kind of unconscious social competition that goes on between one's in-group and any group outside it. According to Tajfel, we humans divide ourselves into social groups through a normal cognitive process that we do not consciously control (Tajfel & Turner, 1986). Much as we classify birds or shoes or the weather into types and categories, our minds automatically divide the expanse of humanity into separate categories known as *social groups*. This process is called *social categorization*. Social categorization enables the formation of social identity. *Social identity* is a sense of who we are based on the social groups we feel we belong to. According to social identify theory, social categorization is inherently an evaluative process, that is, a judgmental one. An individual's social identity carries an emotional and valuational significance. We compare social groups on a spectrum of value, with exalted groups on one end and denigrated groups on the other.

Further, and still by dint of an unconscious process, we exaggerate the merits of our own social identity groups, or in-groups, and overstate the faults of out-groups. Experiments verify that in-groups are perceived as "better" than out-groups in any number of ways deemed important to in-group members: smarter, stronger, more holy, more beautiful, more deserving, more artistic, more practical, funnier, cooler, nicer, ad nauseum (Goldstein, 2002). Why do we do this—judge different social groups to be of unequal value and put our own at the top?

According to social identity theory, we are motivated to elevate our own identity groups because this rewards us with a flattering self-concept (Tajfel & Turner, 1986). So, you see, in-group favoritism and out-group discrimination are the unfortunate results of a social competition that is involuntary and largely unconscious. The competition we create between our own social identity groups and out-groups is fueled by the need for a positive self-concept.

QUESTIONS FOR REFLECTION

2. What do social groups compete over and why do they compete in this way?
3. Reflect for a moment on your own social identity. Can you spot in-group favoritism and out-group discrimination at work? If you spot it, there is an upside. It puts you in position to examine—and regulate—your own biases.

Social identity theory and RCT juxtapose in an interesting way with the findings from evolutionary biology and neuroscience discussed in Chapter 2. Evolutionary biology shows that as a species, humans have an outstanding capacity and a predisposition to cooperate (Tomasello, 2009). Brain-imaging studies have shown that cooperative behavior lights up the brain's reward circuits (Stallen et al., 2017). The unfortunate caveat is, perhaps, that our predisposition to cooperate pertains only to members of our own social identity groups. There is substantial agreement among social psychologists that in-group favoritism–out-group discrimination is a universal phenomenon, independent of culture (Motyl, 2000). RCT and social identity, as well as everyday life, show that competition and the resulting conflict we experience in groups are rooted deeply in social psychological processes that we are not fully aware of and do not choose.

It is important to note, as we end our discussion of social identity theory, that the need for a positive social identity not only drives social division and hierarchy; paradoxically, it can also motivate positive social change (Tajfel & Turner, 1986). In stratified societies, a privileged dominant culture has outsize ability to decree its own biases and perspectives as objective "truth." Therefore, the dominant group's own biases tend to hold sway at large even among oppressed individuals who may internalize the dominant culture's negative stereotypes. It is a breakthrough for civil rights when marginalized people break free from these stereotypes and claim a positive social identity, even amidst oppressive conditions. Struggles to secure rights commensurate with positive social identity and sense of self-worth are an indicator of social progress.

Because all students need a positive social identity, teaching practices that celebrate all the diverse social identities in a heterogeneous classroom are nurturing. However, in addition, strategies that allow students to connect with one another across the lines of social identity are also important. These promote peace by eliminating the biased perceptions associated with social categorization and in-group-out-group social dynamics.

TREATING GROUP AGGRESSION

Whether competition is over identifiable resources or goods, or a contest over which group is "best," it leads to the same result: shades of hostility that pave the way for aggression.

What can be done? Surely it is helpful to be aware of the cognitive biases we are subject to. Knowing that our brains are fallible enables us to step back, calm down, and entertain multiple perspectives. We can critically examine disparaging attitudes toward the "other" and, through will and grace, expand our ability to love one another. This would be the high road, so often pointed toward but so rarely traveled. Fortunately, we can find ways to deter aggression that utilize social psychology and do not depend on self-reflection, humility, and idealism.

The Superordinate Goal

Numerous approaches to reducing group aggression have been tried. These include isolating adversarial groups, forcing new combinations of group members, mediation, adjudicating differences, and more. None of these methods have proven consistently effective. Some attempts, such as convening group leaders to "talk," often make matters worse (Goldstein, 2002). However, there is a method that has been shown to work: bringing antagonistic groups together through superordinate goals (Goldstein, 2002). A *superordinate goal* is an overarching goal that all participants want to achieve. The concept was first articulated by Sherif (1958), who defines superordinate goals this way:

> [Superordinate goals] are goals which are compelling and appealing to members of two or more groups in conflict, but which cannot be attained by the resources and the energies of the groups separately. In effect they are goals attained only when groups pull together. (p. 395)

In his Robber's Cave summer camp studies, Sherif tested superordinate goals such as repairing canoes, fixing broken water supply equipment, and freeing a stuck truck so collaborators could take a fun trip together (Forbs, 1997). Superordinate goals have been successfully used to treat intergroup hostility in "diverse settings, with diverse types of groups, and in diverse cultures" (Goldstein, 2002, p. 6). Turner (1981) summarized the results of numerous studies. He reports:

> Where conflicting groups come into contact under conditions that embody a series of superordinate goals, cooperative activity towards the goal has a cumulative impact in improving intergroup relations; in reducing social distance, dissipating hostile out-group attitudes and stereotypes, and making future intergroup conflicts less likely. (p. 68)

Superordinate goals are emblematic of cooperative games. In a cooperative game, winning means achieving a superordinate goal. Because cooperative games are a delivery mechanism for superordinate goals, there is a sound theoretical basis for using them to intervene against group aggression.

There is an interesting sidelight here for teachers and other professionals who work in conflict resolution. Cooperative games can be used on a stand-alone basis to reduce aggression. Or they be used in conjunction with other methods to enhance their effectiveness. Sherif (1958) explains this as follows:

> It is true that lines of communication between groups must be opened before prevailing hostility can be reduced. But, if contact between the hostile groups takes place without superordinate goals, the communication channels serve as media for further accusations and recriminations. When contact situations involve superordinate goals, communication is utilized in the direction of reducing conflict in order to attain common goals . . . various measures suggested for the reduction of intergroup conflict—disseminating information, increasing social contact, conferences of leaders—acquire new significance and effectiveness when they become part and parcel of interaction processes between groups oriented toward superordinate goals which have real and compelling value for all groups concerned. (p. 356)

Sherif showed that as long as the superordinate goal is enticing, adversaries will be motivated to cooperate. And once they begin to cooperate, the prosocial dynamics of cooperation can begin to work their magic, and the risk of aggression fades. Cooperation is the key.

QUESTION FOR REFLECTION

4. Make up or think of a cooperative game that you already know. Does the game have a superordinate goal? If so, what is it?

The Contact Hypothesis

Gordon Allport (1954) was another midcentury American sociologist who studied conditions that facilitate constructive intergroup contact. Allport agreed that superordinate goals can bring adversarial groups together cooperatively. But in his *contact hypothesis*, he identified several other factors as well. Allport wrote (as cited in Goldstein, 2002, p. 124):

> Prejudice may be reduced by equal status contact between . . . groups in pursuit of common goals. The effect is greatly enhanced if this contact is sanctioned by

institutional supports (i.e., by law, custom, or local atmosphere) . . . (Allport, 1954, p. 281)

Allport's studies, along with those by Sherif and others, produced tangible results. Their findings were quoted in the social science statement that accompanied the brief to the Supreme Court in the *Brown v. Board of Education* landmark case against racial segregation (Goldstein, 2002). Subsequent research has identified even more conditions that mitigate conflict and aggression among rival groups as they make contact. A list of these contact conditions is given below (Goldstein, 2002). Contact should be:

- Cooperative, not competitive.
- Involve superordinate goals.
- Occur repeatedly rather than just once.
- Occur among groups of equal status rather than groups of very different social status.
- Be sanctioned by law, custom, outside authority, and/or institutional norms favoring equality.
- Be intimate rather than superficial.

COOPERATIVE GAMES TO REDUCE GROUP AGGRESSION AT SCHOOL

The social psychology that links competition to aggression helps explain two forms of aggression that occur in school—bullying and ethnocentrism.

Bullying

The U.S. Department of Health and Human Services (n.d.) defines school bullying as "unwanted, aggressive behavior among school aged children that involves a real or perceived power imbalance. The behavior is repeated, or has the potential to be repeated, over time." The document goes on to say, "Bullying includes such actions as making threats, spreading rumors, attacking someone physically or verbally, and excluding someone from a group on purpose." Here we see that exclusion from a group is listed as a form of bullying, right up there with physical assault. Social exclusion is a form of bullying, yet the competitive activities so common in school often involve being excluded from the group. This begs the question: Just how psychologically impactful is the "normal" social exclusion that accompanies competition?

Bullying is usually a form of group aggression (Goldstein, 2002). Typically, the bully does not act alone but is part of a group of aggressors that gangs up on the victim. This explains why feelings of social isolation and rejection are a common reaction to being bullied.

Cooperative games can be the basis of a bullying-prevention program. Bullying prevention is distinguished from "anti-bullying" approaches. The latter emphasizes consequences for aggressive behavior that has already occurred, while the former optimizes school climate to prevent aggression. Both bullying prevention and response are important, but it is easier, more effective, and more humane to stop bullying before it starts. Data on punitive anti-bullying efforts show that they are not generally effective, plus they carry the risk of unintended downsides such as scapegoating and marginalizing students (Bickmore, 2011). In addition, by the time bullying response takes place, the victims have already been harmed. Preventing bullying by maintaining a positive climate is the most strategic approach.

My 2015 book, *The Cooperative Games Bullying Prevention Program*, presents a research-based method to use the games for this purpose. The method involves using the same series of cooperative games that were tested in the University of Nevada study that I have mentioned previously (Bay-Hinitz et al., 1994). The researchers reported unambiguous findings with the games they tested, stating: "Results showed that cooperative behavior increased, and aggression decreased during cooperative games; conversely, competitive games were followed by increases in aggressive behavior and decreases in cooperative behavior" (p. 60). The study offers a model for implementing cooperative games that can be emulated. By using the same games that were used in the study and using them in the same manner, the teacher can reasonably expect similar results.

Seven active cooperative games were tested in the Reno study, and directions for all these games are provided in this book. The seven active games are Cooperative Musical Chairs, Freeze DeFreeze Tag, Balance Activities, Cooperative Musical Hugs, Devine, Half a Heart, and Beanbag Freeze (see Chapter 4 for all the games except Beanbag Freeze, which is at the end of this chapter.) All of these games were developed by Terry Orlick (2006). Four board games were also tested. These are Max, Sleeping Grump, Granny's House, and Harvest Time. All of these were designed by Jim Deacove (personal communication, January 21, 2021).

A few comments are in order about the distinguishing features of these particular games, for it cannot be assumed that all cooperative games will have the same social effects. Though all the games that were tested are fun and exciting, and several of them are plenty silly as well, they have a gentle quality. For example, the narrative of the board game Max involves a big tomcat named Max sleeping on a porch and a group of small creatures (a mouse, chipmunk, and bird) trying to complete a journey to their "home tree." Max has one eye open, however, and cats need to eat too, so he is a threat! Instead of vilifying Max, players strategize how to use tokens—milk, cheese, catnip—to lure him back to the porch. Coexistence and problem-solving are taught, rather than us-versus-them thinking. The game Harvest

Time involves picking vegetables before winter comes and helping neighbors when there is a surplus. Sleeping Grump is a suspenseful game in which players try to climb a beanstalk to recapture belongings that had been stolen by the slumbering giant. In the end, players take back their belongings but leave a little bit of their treasure for Grump so that when he wakes, he may learn kindness. To best replicate the Reno study's findings, I recommend using board games with sensitive and inclusive messages such as these. For aggression prevention, avoid games with narratives that force players to coordinate to defeat a villain. Even if the competition is against fictitious characters on the game board, it still rallies the players to aggressive action.

In the Reno study, children were not required to participate in any game and could leave at any time they wished (Bay-Hinitz et al., 1994). The choice to opt out is probably critically important. High motivation is key to cooperative gaming, and if students are forced to play, they are not going to be highly motivated. Recall from Chapter 1 that forcing someone to play violates the very definition of play.

The researchers ended their study with the following remarks about using cooperative games to stanch aggression in young children—and thereby decrease its prevalence among adolescent students and beyond:

> Aggressive behaviors in children and adolescents have become an increasingly serious problem . . . To the degree that the roots of aggression lie in failure to learn and practice positive social behaviors in early childhood, preschool environments that promote the widespread use of cooperative games (coupled with limitations on competitive games) may reduce tendencies to respond aggressively and may positively affect future behavior. (Bay-Hinitz et al., 1994, p. 445)

Ethnocentrism

The term *ethnocentrism* was defined in 1906 by sociologist William Sumner as: "the technical name for the view of things in which one's own group is the center of everything . . . [whereby] Each group nourishes its own pride and vanity, boasts itself superior, exalts its own divinities, and looks with contempt on outsiders" (p. 13). Today, ethnocentrism has a second, more specific meaning: Ethnocentrism is "an ethnic or cultural interpretation of the more general process of in-group—out-group differentiation. Ethnocentrism combines a positive attitude toward one's own ethnic/cultural group (the in-group) with a negative attitude toward other ethnic/cultural groups (the out-group)" (Motyl, 2000, pp. 152–153).

Thus, ethnocentrism is the same toxic group dynamic of in-group favoritism and out-group discrimination that stems from intergroup competition and leads to hostility, as RCT has described. But in the case of ethnocentrism, the intergroup prejudice and conflict occurs among cultural and ethnic groups.

Ethnocentrism is a conspicuous social force in societies everywhere, certainly including the United States at the time of this writing. Racial, ethnic, and gender-based prejudice, discrimination, and hate are its calling cards. Social division, high-stakes political competition, and a long history of racism, sexism, social hierarchies, and various forms of discrimination are among its causes and effects.

As we have been discussing, cooperative games are used successfully as an intervention for hostility and aggression related to intergroup bias (Goldstein, 1999). Insofar as ethnocentrism is a special case of intergroup bias, it follows that cooperative games can mitigate it, too. Especially at this moment in history, when ethnocentrism is such a clear threat to peace and unity, it will be good news if playing together can help to dissolve it. More studies are urgently needed.

If your intention is to use cooperative games to reduce intergroup friction rooted in ethnocentrism, here are a few recommendations to consider:

1. *Choose appropriate superordinate goals.* Apply the general rule that superordinate goals must appeal to all participants (Sherif, 1958). To do this, look for superordinate goals that do not have a strong cultural flavor and that are appealing and relatable to everyone.
2. *Alternatively, celebrate multiculturalism in an obvious way and choose culturally expressive superordinate goals.* In this case, introduce a variety of games reflecting different cultural traditions. Be sure every student sees themselves in some of the games you have chosen for the group. Take care to avoid stereotypical or marginalizing expressions of culture to be sure all players feel included, respected, and welcome.
3. *Apply the conditions of favorable group contact.* The games you choose should feature:
   » *Cooperative Contact.* To assure this, verify that the games you choose involve positive interdependence. Everyone knows they must depend on everyone else to win.
   » *Multiple Contacts.* That is, play cooperative games repeatedly if the goal is to improve intergroup relations.
   » *Support of Relevant Authorities.* Try to enlist the support of fellow teachers, administrators, and parents and other influential community members in your cooperative games effort. Interventions work best when they have visible institutional support.
   » *Intimate Contact.* The games should get participants mingling and interacting sincerely with one another. Perfunctory contact does not break down the walls we build around ourselves.
4. *Apply the principles of culturally responsive pedagogy and equitable practices.* In your teaching with cooperative games, be

sensitive about triggering trauma related to racism, misogyny, and other forms of cultural persecution. Avoid any board game with a narrative that reflects cultural stereotypes, of course, or demeans or objectifies anyone.

5. *Handle social identities with care.* From the point of view of an individual, a strong social identity can be a necessary protective device as well as a source of great pride and sense of belonging. So, as you work with in-group–out-group dynamics, focus on reducing out-group discrimination first. Do not expect students to be self-critical about any in-group biases they may hold.

6. *Choose games that allow participants with different social identities to develop empathy for one another.* For example, the Beanbag Freeze game described below gives players the chance to feel what any other "frozen" player feels like, and to respond with empathy, across boundaries of social identity.

   This is important because recent evidence indicates that when in-group members feel empathy for one another, their empathy does not necessarily extend to people outside their own social group. Indeed, some evidence shows that the *more* empathy in-group members have for one another, the *less* likely they are to help out-group members and the more disposed they are to harm them (Bruneau, Cikara, & Saxe, 2017). Teaching empathy is not enough! Methods to help students develop empathy for people *outside their own social groups* are needed for peace.

7. *Last, don't forget the basics.* Of course, choose games that are age-appropriate. Use the guidelines for facilitators discussed in Chapter 5.

CHAPTER SUMMARY

Aggression is behavior that intentionally causes physical or psychological injury to another person. Students are aggressive in school for numerous reasons, including biological factors, lack of knowledge of prosocial skills and values, and competition. Cooperative games are used to treat aggressive individuals in therapeutic situations and in schools.

Group aggression takes many forms, from hazing to bullying to riots to wars. The suffering and existential threat that group aggression entails cannot be overstated. The foundational theory of human aggression, realistic conflict theory, identifies competition over social or material goods as the ultimate source of human aggression. Social identity theory modifies realistic conflict theory by pointing to competition for top status in social hierarchies as another cause of group aggression.

In-group–out-group perception is part and parcel of the competitive mindset. Intergroup conflict is reduced when groups share a superordinate goal. Games with a superordinate goal, that is, cooperative games, have been used as an intervention to reduce in-group favoritism and out-group discrimination, hostility, and violence. The games can be used on their own or in combination with other conflict reduction strategies. When cooperative games are combined with other peace-promoting strategies, the effectiveness of those other strategies increases.

Bullying and ethnocentrism (which is in-group favoritism and out-group discrimination in a cultural or ethnic context) are two kinds of group aggression that occur in schools. Cooperative games help prevent bullying by reducing aggressive behavior, and by promoting a positive classroom climate where bullying is unlikely to take root. The theoretical rationale for using cooperative games to abate ethnocentrism is that the games bring students together under constructive contact conditions, disrupting us-versus-them rivalry. More research into these important applications of cooperative games is needed.

A more widely recognized application of cooperative games is early childhood education, the subject of the next chapter. The practice is thriving, as you will see.

QUESTION FOR REFLECTION

5. True or False: Competition is the root of us-versus-them thinking, and us-versus-them thinking is the root of group aggression.

PLAY TO LEARN—TRY THIS!

BEANBAG FREEZE

This game can be played indoors or outside. It takes about 20 minutes. Groups of 4 or more can play. It is best for children ages 5 and up. Materials needed: one beanbag per student; a music source such as a CD player.

Directions:

- Give each student a beanbag and ask him to balance it on his head (see Figure 8.1).
- Turn the music on and ask students to move slowly about the play area, keeping the beanbag on their head. They can walk or move in any silly or fun way they please.

- Now ask the students to pick up the pace and move more actively—hopping, skipping, turning, and so forth, all the while balancing the beanbag on their heads.
- If a player loses his beanbag, he is frozen until another player picks it up and places it back on his head. If the helper also loses her beanbag, she too is frozen until another friend comes to thaw them both by replacing their beanbags. (Very young children can hold their beanbags in place on their heads while they help their friends.) Be sure to tell the players that the point of the game is to help their classmates by replacing fallen beanbags so they can stay in the game. The game ends when everyone has been thawed or everyone is frozen or tired.

Figure 8.1. Beanbag Freeze creates an atmosphere of caring and collaboration where personal differences and social divisions are irrelevant and fade from view.

CHAPTER 9

Cooperative Games in Early Childhood Education

All I really need to know, I learned in kindergarten.

—Robert Fulghum

Jim Deacove, the creator of the world's first cooperative board games, was introduced earlier in this book. He has been designing and manufacturing games through his small business, Family Pastimes, in Canada for over 40 years. In an interview, I asked Jim how he got started. He explained:

Well, the making of cooperative games came about out of a family need. When the girls were small and beginning to play games, [my wife] Ruth and I were not happy about all the squabbling that took place over winning and losing. We thought we were lacking in parenting skills but found that if you changed the rules of the game, you got different behavior. We played Scrabble with a family score. We suddenly saw the same behavior as when we worked together in the garden. And then when I couldn't find any sharing games in any stores, necessity became the father of invention. Over the past 40 years, I have been hearing from teachers all over the world about how games like Max and Harvest Time have helped in the classroom, especially with young children. Oh, my. There are lotsa, lotsa reasons why! Bonding, support, playfulness, teamwork, shared decision-making, openness, trust, safety, self-worth, personal power, well-being, realizing all academic goals. These are just a few of the things that come to mind.

—Jim Deacove (personal communication, January 21, 2021)

YOUNG CHILDREN AND PLAY

If you have spent any time with children or thought about your own childhood, you know that children do not need to be taught how to play. Children start playing on their own as infants (Gray, 2013). Unless they are blocked by illness or oppressive conditions, they keep playing all the way through childhood. Children take to play in the same way that they begin to crawl, walk, or talk. Any behavior that shows up this naturally and universally must surely be rooted in the deepest levels of the human being (Carlsson-Paige, 2018). Indeed, the urge to play must be even more deeply rooted in us than our specifically human faculties, because so many other animals play while young as well.

Why do children, and in fact young dolphins, parrots, deer, whales, dogs, cats, and other intelligent animals, play? In terms of evolutionary biology, its purpose seems clear intuitively: Play prepares youth for adulthood (Lents, 2017). Through play, the young learn how to be in the world. It is a process of learning skills, norms, and information about oneself and the social and physical environments. Play deprivation is extremely harmful to children and threatens all aspects of their development—social, emotional, cognitive, and physical (Goldstein, 2012).

Recall from Chapter 1 that play is an active, engaging, and voluntary activity that is nonliteral and produces feelings of well-being such as fun, joy, or contentment and where outcome does not matter (F. Hughes, 2010). With this definition, we see that children are playing when they draw pictures, wrestle, dress up, talk to an imaginary friend, pound a lump of clay, drive a toy car, splash in a puddle, or set up a lemonade stand. Different children play in different ways, expressing their temperaments, talents, and cultural influences. However, recurring patterns in play are discernible.

Types of Play

Play can be classified in various ways. Table 9.1 shows a taxonomy of play types useful to early childhood educators, parents, and play workers (B. Hughes, 2002). This classification is not an exhaustive list. It is something like a field guide, helping us recognize play when we see it, and calling attention to facets of common play behaviors.

Cooperative play is normal, natural, and free. Notice how few of these types of play involve competition. Based on this taxonomy, the most common source of competition in childhood play is games with competitive rules. Because most types of play can be engaged in cooperatively or individually, it is really quite easy for teachers to foster play without encouraging competition in the classroom.

QUESTION FOR REFLECTION

1. Children sometimes like to compare their physical abilities to one another, for example, by running races or jumping contests. How can you help children engage in this type of activity with a cooperative mindset?

Table 9.1. A Taxonomy of Play Types

Social Play	Imaginative Play	Rough-and-Tumble Play	Locomotor Play
Players interact with others through explicit rules, as in playing games or running a race.	Players pretend that natural laws and conventional rules do not apply, as in pretending to fly.	Players are in energetic and close contact with each other that is not violent, as in tickling and wrestling.	Players move for the sheer joy of it, as in dancing, twirling around, and doing somersaults.
Sociodramatic Play	**Fantasy Play**	**Creative Play**	**Exploratory Play**
Players act out real-world experiences they have had or may have later, such as playing house or pretending to be a firefighter.	Players construct a fantasy world and take on roles unavailable in real life, such as king, dragon, or astronaut.	Players make new things, develop new ideas, or use original insight to transform their surroundings.	Players use their senses to obtain factual information about objects, places, etc., such as mouthing their toys.
Dramatic Play	**Communication Play**	**Mastery Play**	**Recapitulative Play**
Players dramatize events they have not participated in, for example, being stranded on an island.	Players use words or gestures, as in telling jokes, singing, and rhyming.	Players attempt to control the physical or affective environment, as in building a raft to cross a stream.	Players explore history, rituals, stories, or myths, as in building a castle or dressing up like Cleopatra.
Object Play	**Symbolic Play**	**Deep Play**	**Role Play**
Players use their senses and hand-eye coordination to understand objects, as in squeezing play dough and using lacing cards.	Players use an object or action to represent a different real-world object, action, or idea, as when a stick becomes an airplane.	Players experience intense feelings of ecstasy, thrill, transcendence, or fear, as might happen when riding a horse.	Players enact roles or activities not of a significant social or personal nature, such as ironing clothes, tying a shoe, or using a shovel.

Source: B. Hughes, 2002.

COOPERATIVE PLAY—THE CAPSTONE OF EARLY
CHILDHOOD SOCIAL DEVELOPMENT

The term *cooperative play* was introduced to the social sciences by psychologist Mildred Parten (1932) nearly 100 years ago. Although Parten's work is from another era, her basic insights are still guiding lights and are widely accepted (F. Hughes, 2010).

In her Theory of Play Stages, Parten described six stages of play that children progress through from birth to age six. These six stages are summarized in Table 9.2. The stages show that there is a progression toward increasing social participation as children grow older. The final stage of social development is reached through and reflected by cooperative play. In the cooperative play stage, children engage with peers toward a purpose such as making a creative product, dramatizing situations, or playing a game with rules. Prior to this stage, children are not able to coordinate with one

Table 9.2 Parten's Stages of Play

Typical Age	Type of Play	Description of Play
0–3 mos.	Unoccupied Play	The child does not play but occupies himself by paying attention to things of momentary interest. He may play with his own body, sit in one spot, or follow a parent or teacher around the room.
3 mos.– 2 yrs.	Solitary Play	The child plays alone with objects but not people. She is engrossed in her own world and does not acknowledge other children.
2–2.5 yrs.	Onlooker Play	The child watches other children play with interest and may make comments to other children, but he does not engage himself.
2.5–3 yrs.	Parallel Play	Children play beside each other, aware of the activities of one another. They may use the same play materials, but each child still plays separately.
3–4 yrs.	Associative Play	Each child remains focused on a separate activity, but there is sharing, taking turns, lending, growing interest in peers, and expanding communication.
4–6 yrs.	Cooperative Play	Children play with others in groups of 2 or more. They coordinate with their peers toward agreed-upon goals and methods of play. Social skills get a lot of practice, and friendships form. Social interaction can be complex. Games with rules can be played. Dramatic role-playing is a popular activity.

Sources: Parten, 1932; F. Hughes, 2010.

another in complex ways (Parten, 1932). Thus, it is through cooperative play that children learn how to participate fully in social groups. That is how vital cooperative play is to children.

The common view among modern psychologists is that Parten's framework needs a few modifications. It is now known that children do not move from one play stage to the next in an inexorable, linear progression. Instead, healthy maturation involves doubling back to revisit earlier stages even as the general trend is toward more complex and more social play (F. Hughes, 2010). It is true that a preference for solitary play can be a sign of social immaturity in an older child, but usually it is not. The 5-year-old who spends endless hours drawing, or observing nature, or doing cartwheels, is probably cultivating a talent rather than expressing an inability to get along with others. Or he may have an introverted temperament and an especially rich inner life. Also, it is now understood that Parten underestimated the ability of toddlers to play cooperatively. Children as young as 18 months can play in simple, socially coordinated ways. For example, toddlers may take turns in peekaboo and chasing games (F. Hughes, 2010).

QUESTION FOR REFLECTION

2. The following observation of nursery children at play was made by Mildred Parten (1932, p. 251). Which stage of play was she observing?

"Several children are engaged in filling cups in a sandbox. Each child has his own cup and fills it without references to what the other children are doing with their cups. There is very little conversation about what they are making. The children play beside one another rather than with each other."

HOW COOPERATIVE PLAY PROMOTES SOCIAL DEVELOPMENT

Playing together, especially through highly interactive cooperative play, poses real challenges to the child. As Parten described (1932), cooperative play requires give-and-take, accommodation, and negotiation. When cooperative play commences, children are still very self-centered cognitively, as pointed out in Chapter 1. Piaget's theory of cognitive development explains that children between the ages of 2 and 7 are in the preoperational stage of cognitive development. During this stage, children are unable to see situations from another's point of view (McLeod, 2018). This set of circumstances can make for a bumpy ride when children try to play together, but it is richly educational: Cooperative play "is the most highly organized group activity in which appears the elements of division of labor, group censorship, centralization of control in the hands of one or two members, and the subordination of individual desire to that of the group" (Parten, 1932, p. 250).

This description of cooperative play from Parten shows that it includes all manner of socially coordinated play, including play that may not be especially prosocial. Despite the bumps and bruises children endure, the process is essential to their social growth. Mastering the nuances of playing well with others is a complex and subtle art that may take a lifetime of practice. Children need not become masters by age 5, but baseline competence is necessary to function smoothly in typical kindergarten settings.

Teachers support cooperative play development by giving children plenty of opportunity to engage in it. Support for prosocial behavioral choices can be provided in an unobtrusive way. Though children need to learn through their own experimentation and discovery, teacher supervision is important because children can hurt each other physically and emotionally. If children experience serious aggression, exclusion, or rejection by their peers in this formative stage, healthy social development can be set back (Orlick, 1978).

Sociodramatic Play

To understand the psychology of cooperative play, consider the form most prevalent among young children—sociodramatic play. Sociodramatic play involves children playing various everyday roles while they engage in make-believe action sequences (F. Hughes, 2010). A timeless example is playing house. Sociodramatic play has more impact on young children's developing social awareness than any other kind of play (Hartley, Frank, & Goldenson, 1952, in F. Hughes, 2010). This is because imaginary, yet realistic role-playing requires children to keenly observe, remember, and practice patterns of social interaction. Further, sociodramatic play requires intricate communication, since players must relay to others what they envision in their own heads. Even more impressively, sociodramatic cooperative play involves coordination with the behaviors of a partner. Such coordination requires children to understand the *social rules* (norms, customs, taboos, laws, etc.) that define appropriate behavior in a particular cultural setting. The child must understand these social rules even when they are not made explicit. Taking turns is an example of a social rule young children need to internalize and be able to use. People of every age, including adults, need to be aware of the social rules that apply in any social context in order to gain social acceptance in that context (F. Hughes, 2010).

Vygotsky and Social Rules

The Russian theorist Lev Vygotsky, known for his sociocultural theory of play, emphasized how important it is for children to learn social rules through their play. His theory is too richly detailed and intellectually abstract to delve into fully here, but you can understand the gist of it through a scenario you can probably relate to. Imagine you work in a busy workplace and you are having a conversation with your employer. In this interaction, a social rule that is likely to pertain is that you should speak succinctly. Now, suppose you are in mid-explanation, but your boss starts looking at her watch. Because you understand the applicable social rule (to be succinct) and the cultural "sign" or "symbol" representing it (watch-checking), you finish up your comments quickly. Because you have applied the right social rule, you stay in the good graces of your boss. Can you see how sociodramatic play helps children prepare for the social challenges they will face as they grow? Playacting adult roles, such as "boss and worker," "mommy and daddy," or "clerk and customer," gives children the chance to focus on and practice using social rules.

Cooperative Play and Making Friends

There are many other ways that cooperative play helps children grow socially as well. It helps them understand that there is a difference between their own thoughts and feelings and those of others. This realization improves their ability to interact with other people, imagine multiple viewpoints, and empathize (Burns & Brainerd, 1979). Further, competence in cooperative play helps children develop friendships. Research shows that preschoolers who are well-liked by their peers engage in a lot of cooperative play. Being unable to participate in sustained cooperative play, on the other hand, is a risk factor for rejection by peers. Fortunately, it is possible to help socially withdrawn or unpopular children by coaching them in the social skills needed for group acceptance, such as listening to others, sharing, and offering ideas. Cooperative play is a common vehicle for teaching socially awkward children how to improve their social proficiency (F. Hughes, 2010).

TWO DEFINITIONS OF COOPERATIVE PLAY

In terms of Parten's Theory of Play Stages, "cooperative play" is a type of play that reflects the most advanced stage of social development in young children. Interestingly, Parten (1932) included competitive play in her definition of cooperative play. She said so explicitly, stating that cooperative play can be "organized for the purpose of . . . striving to attain some competitive goal" (p. 251).

The phrase "cooperative play" has a very different meaning outside of Parten's lexicon. As we know, the term "cooperative play" today is understood as play that is devoid of competition. It can include noncompetitive play or fully cooperative play (i.e., play requiring cooperative skills and featuring positive interdependence). But it never includes competition. In this book, as in popular culture, cooperative play is understood in this latter sense. Cooperative games are a subset of this kind of cooperative play. They are formal games with rules that require cooperation. Their rules require players to work together and thereby experience cooperation. Further, today's cooperative games (at least those that align with the definition supplied by the midcentury cooperative games movement) involve fully prosocial cooperation—cooperation that is inclusive and benign.

There is no doubt that today's cooperative play and games fall within the scope of Parten's sixth stage of play. They are quintessentially cooperative. Parten's well-accepted theory, and the decades of research supporting it, therefore help make the case that the cooperative games and play we recognize today are developmentally appropriate and important as educational tools for young children.

Parten's language leaves us with some questions about the role of competitive play on social development, however. Why did she not distinguish among cooperative and competitive play as separate forces on children's social development? We know, on the basis of the many arguments and studies discussed in this book, that it is an important distinction. Culture, time, and place would largely explain Parten's choice. She was working in the 1930s, a time in American history when the competitive ethos dominated the national mood (Goldstein, 1999). In this environment, she would have never heard "the case against competition," as Alfie Kohn puts it (1986). Parten's work preceded all of the groundbreaking midcentury social-psychological research by Deutsch and others that showed, definitively, that competition and cooperation have opposite social effects.

Now, nearly 100 years after Parten's time, we understand the social development of children in much more refined terms. We have the benefit of decades of research on cooperation and competition, as well as the importance of social-emotional learning, which Parten did not have. So we thank Mildred Parten for her keen observations of play stages and her insight into the importance of cooperative play, but we press on to explore the fork in the road she could not see.

SUMMARY OF IMPORTANT DIFFERENCES BETWEEN COMPETITIVE AND COOPERATIVE PLAY

We know that children do not have an inherent need to engage in competitive play to develop into socially mature adults. Anthropological research has shown that there are entire societies where children never engage in competitive play at all (F. Hughes, 2010). These competition-free societies are marked by peacefulness and long-term sustainability (Kohn, 1986).

Though Parten's theory does not distinguish among competitive and cooperative play, the theory, research, and logic explored in this book show that it is an important distinction. To recap some of the evidence and arguments: Social interdependence theory tells us that competition undermines productive and peaceful social interaction (Deutsch, 1949b). Also, the many insights presented in Chapter 3 warn that competition correlates to lowered self-esteem, increased anxiety, and other deleterious effects specifically for children. Other studies (Bay-Hinitz et al., 1994) with young children demonstrate that competitive school activities decrease prosocial behavior and increase aggression in the classroom. Also, the insights and observations of Cornelius and Lentz (1950), educators behind the earliest known writing on cooperative games, indicate that competitive play is emotionally harmful to children and teaches an aggressive mindset. In this same vein, two of the theorists of group aggression we have discussed at length in Chapter 8—namely Goldstein and Sherif—studied the effects of competition on children. Their research-based conclusion is that competition sets up hostility, us-versus-them group dynamics, and intergroup bias, and can lead to aggression (Goldstein, 2002; Sherif, 1958.) Indeed, as pointed out in Chapter 1, Maria Montessori stated that teaching young children to compete in school is tantamount to preparing them for war. The emotional meltdowns that young children often display when they lose in a competitive game is an everyday indicator that competitive games are not developmentally suitable for young children. The California Preschool Curriculum Framework concurs when it says, "Overly competitive games can work against community caring and collaborative learning and should be avoided" (California Department of Education, 2013, p. 81).

The purpose of this book is not to argue that competition has no role in early childhood education. Certainly, the intent is not to shame the many kind and caring people who regularly engage in competition and profess their enjoyment of it. Rather, the goal is to present the rationale for educating with cooperative games. This involves critical examination of popular notions about competition. The truth is that competition is so firmly entrenched in our society and educational system that extricating it completely from the classroom may be impossible. And perhaps there can be value in teaching children how to compete in relatively benign ways. Chapter 3 offers some ideas for doing this, including emphasizing social rules of fair play, using the concept of personal best, and keeping competitive stakes low. But because cooperative play is clearly so essential and competitive play so full of risks, we are left to conclude that playing together, not against each other, is the preferred path to social maturity for young children.

QUESTIONS FOR REFLECTION

3. How does Parten's definition of cooperative play differ from the definition that is used in most other contexts?
4. Why is it important for teachers to distinguish among the effects of cooperative versus competitive play on children's development?

HOW TO USE COOPERATIVE GAMES IN THE EARLY CHILDHOOD CLASSROOM

Use the following list of practical recommendations as a menu. Choose what works best for your setting, and have fun!

Select Developmentally Appropriate Cooperative Games and Play Activities

Provide opportunities for cooperative play and games that are neither too easy nor too challenging. Aim for the zone of proximal development (as explained in Chapter 1), so children can refine emerging skills (Vygotsky, 1930).

1. Toddlers are generally too young to engage in cooperative play on their own, but you can engage them in simple adult-directed cooperative play activities such as peekaboo or simple catching or chasing games. The simplest clapping games are another enjoyable cooperative play activity that an adult can engage in with toddlers. Also, helping toddlers learn how to assist one another with simple tasks, to be gentle to animals, to care for plants, to take turns with toys, to lend and share resources, and to pass items around a circle are all good precursors to cooperative play because they teach wee ones to be gentle and helpful.

2. Group projects involving parallel or associative play are a great way to get 3- or 4-year-olds ready for later cooperative play. For example, children can color different portions of a mural or contribute different objects to an imaginary bowl of soup.

3. If you are working with children who have reached the cooperative play stage, provide plenty of opportunities for sociodramatic play. Props can make sociodramatic play extra fun and enticing. Props that literally represent a social role (for example, a toy stethoscope) can elicit engagement but also constrain children's imaginations and creativity. So less literal props are recommended as well—things like boxes, blankets, ribbons, and such (F. Hughes, 2010).

4. Introduce cooperative board games only after children have become proficient with cooperative play. Games with formal rules, including board games, generally require social and cognitive skills beyond the ability of toddlers.

Become a Skilled Cooperative Games Facilitator

Take your role as a cooperative play facilitator seriously. Cooperative games can provide many teachable moments. But there is much for you to do! Refer to the guidelines for facilitators discussed at length in Chapter 5.

Support Cooperative Free Play

Unstructured play that children choose and direct themselves, termed *free play*, is the bedrock of early childhood development (Carlsson-Paige, 2018). Honor it by giving it plenty of time and space. Without being obtrusive, do what you can to plant the seeds for prosocial free play. Once children are able to play well together, rather than fight and compete, they can help one another discover the joys of cooperation under the sunny skies of a positive classroom climate. You can support socially constructive, cooperative free play in several ways:

1. Encourage cooperation-infused free play by providing toys and props that facilitate it. Puppets, puzzles, tea sets, merry-go-rounds, and playhouses are good cooperative toys.
2. Provide play opportunities that facilitate a wide range of social participation. Certain kinds of play materials and activities—blocks, clay, musical instruments, creative movement, and sociodramatic play—can help timid and socially immature children participate in group play. These activities allow social participation but do not force it by allowing children to wade into group situations to the extent they are comfortable.
3. Show children that cooperation is fun by playing teacher-led cooperative games with them. Once children are exposed to the joy of cooperation through games, they are more likely to take part in prosocial, cooperative play in their free play periods (Orlick, 1981).
4. Reinforce norms of cooperation and inclusivity to establish a cooperative classroom climate, as discussed further below. Decorate the room with posters illustrating cooperative themes. Pictures of animals of different species playing together are perfect. You will discover that free play is likely to reflect the cooperative milieu you have cultivated in your classroom.

Use Cooperative Games to Teach Academic Subjects

If the aim is teaching academic subjects to children age 6 and under, the pedagogical framework called *guided play* is useful (Toub et al., 2016). Refer to Chapter 1 for more details on the guided play approach.

Use Cooperative Games for Social-Emotional Learning

You can use cooperative games to integrate SEL throughout the school day or as the centerpiece of an SEL program (refer to Chapter 7 for more detailed information).

Use Cooperative Games for Inclusion

Everyone knows how bad it feels to be excluded from a group we want to be a part of. It feels like rejection, and young children are very sensitive to it (F. Hughes, 2010). Cooperative games are inclusive by their very nature. Use them as a tool to set a norm of inclusion. When you do, you will be fulfilling a major directive of SEL and nurturing a positive classroom climate, which helps to prevent bullying (Lyons, 2015). Here are a few tips for fostering inclusion with cooperative play.

1. When leading the entire class, avoid games that are too complex for your least capable students. Games with simple directions can be equally fun for everyone. Cooperative games pioneer and authority Terry Orlick (2006) has said that all truly cooperative games are inclusive. If games are too complex for all children to access, they cannot be inclusive.
2. Play different kinds of cooperative games that speak to different tastes, talents, and abilities. Use games that involve singing or music, active games that showcase locomotive skills, games that center on verbal skills, and so on to be sure that all children feel included.
3. To be sure the games you choose are accessible to all children, you need to modify rules and make accommodations for children with special needs. It is in keeping with the spirit of cooperative games to be flexible and responsive to student preferences and needs. Avoid rigidity. Stay loose. Modify games in a joyful way to communicate how welcome everyone is in the group.
4. Make inclusion a game rule. For example, in Balloon Bop each child must touch and pass the balloon to another child for the group to win as a whole.
5. Watch for exclusionary behavior. Any signs that a child is feeling humiliated, shamed, or sidelined must be attended to right away. Do this through distraction, with rule changes, and/or by empowering the targeted child by giving her public praise. Also, discuss exclusive behavior with children who demonstrate it, explaining that special friends are nice but being kind and caring to everyone is important, too. Group game time is not the time for special friends to be alone, but for everyone to be friendly to one another so no one feels left out.
6. Open communication is a feature of inclusive classrooms (Sapon-Shevin, 2007). Students should feel relaxed and comfortable talking about how they are alike and how they are different. You can model this by referring to individual differences in a natural and accepting way. With sensitivity, find ways to acknowledge and show

support for attributes that can be marginalizing, such as language differences. Use cooperative games to unify the class amidst the diversity you openly celebrate.

7. Following on the above, teach open and gentle communication skills. Use the games to do this. The best cooperative games elicit prosocial communication skills such as sharing ideas, providing help and encouragement, listening to others, and asking for help.

8. In an inclusive classroom, children feel that they are accepted and belong to the group just as they are. Contests "proving" that some children are "better" than others are not consistent with inclusion. Look for ways to praise children for attributes that society may not celebrate enough. Instead of harping on how smart or cute children are, praise them for being funny, for showing kindness, for taking care of school property, for being on time, for having a fun hairstyle, for having lots of energy, for listening quietly, and so forth. See and celebrate individual strengths.

Use Cooperative Games for Trauma-Sensitive Practice

Childhood trauma and neglect can impair the developing brains of young children (Gaskill & Perry, 2014). This neurological damage makes it harder for maltreated children to function in the classroom and learn the skills and concepts that their teachers so earnestly want to teach them.

The neurosequential model of education (NME) developed by Bruce Perry explains the neuroscience underlying the symptoms of toxic stress. Perry is a psychiatrist and researcher, the senior fellow at the Child Trauma Academy in Houston, and a professor at the Feinberg School of Medicine in Chicago, Illinois. According to the NME, a history of trauma can leave a child with an overactive *stress response system,* that is, hyperexcited neural networks in the lower parts of the brain that regulate response to threat. These neural networks operate on continuous high alert, keeping the child in a perpetual state of perceived threat. In this state, the cortical region of the brain—the brain structures associated with reason, thought, language, empathy, and other capacities we recognize as "intelligent" or distinctly human—cannot be accessed. The child's behavior is impulsive, chaotic, and unregulated. She may be actively disruptive and highly agitated (Rizzi, 2021).

According to Perry, play therapy is appropriate treatment for such children (Gaskill & Perry, 2014). Perry recommends games that can be played in gentle and supportive ways. The gentlest games are cooperative games, so it can be inferred that these are the games most consistent with the NME.

Trauma-sensitive teaching practice involves using strategies that help students to intentionally regulate their own nervous systems. As per the

NME, class time should begin with mindfulness practices such as breathing exercises, tapping, or drumming. These activities help students regulate the primitive parts of their brain that react to threat and are chronically over-stimulated. However, students are likely still not calm enough to learn after these techniques. Often, children affected by trauma feel so fearful around other people that they cannot think and learn effectively in a classroom setting. Class activities that make students feel relationally safe are needed. Cooperative games, being gentle, kind, and inclusive, are perfectly suited for this role. Cooperative play activities, such as dancing, painting a mural, or building a tower of blocks, help everyone—children who suffer from trauma and those who don't—feel comfortable, accepted, and safe enough in school to think and learn. As this book is being written, social and environmental crises no longer loom over us—they permeate the fabric of our lives. The COVID pandemic, wildfires, the teetering of our democratic foundation, and an always-on media filling today's virtual public square with a steady diet of banality, divisive lies, and verbal violence are just a few of the disasters that have become our dance partners in these times. Trauma-sensitive educational practices have been de-veloped to address the acute problems that children suffering from toxic stress experience in school. Their needs are paramount. However, truly, trauma in some degree has become a feature of everyday life for most if not all teachers and students. We all benefit from, if not need, practices that help us regulate our nervous systems for calm and focus. And we need practices that create relationally safe environments, like playing cooperative games.

Play Cooperative Games for Hope

Hope is energy that fuels us forward. Without hope, we have no motivation to do the work needed to create a better world, nor do we have faith that our dreams can someday come true. Cooperative games are a pedagogy that nurtures the kind of hope we need most in these times of crisis—hope in collective action. Well-designed cooperative games give students an experi-ence of achieving collective goals through a respectful, inclusive process in which multiple perspectives and diverse needs and talents are all seen and honored. The games thus counter norms and narratives telling students they must compete or act individually to attain goals. Traditional norms and nar-ratives exalting competition and individualism breed hopelessness because a lone individual striving or competing against others has little realistic ability to surmount complex global problems. "What can *I* do?" and "It's beyond my control" are the ubiquitous expressions of despair and resignation we often hear. The solutions for today's interconnected social and environmen-tal problems demand collective action toward superordinate goals, just as cooperative games model and teach us how to do. It is vital to instill hope in collective action through effective pedagogies such as cooperative games so that today's children grow up knowing that working together works.

Play Cooperative Games for Joy

Buddhist educator, philosopher, and poet Daisaku Ikeda described joy as the "beautiful blossoming of life" that springs from "wonderful encounters" (Ritsuko, 2021). In a similar vein, educator and philosopher Nel Noddings describes joy as an emotion or state of being arising from one's sense of communion with the ones she cares for (Noddings, 1984). In positive psychology, joy is regarded as a component of happiness—and therefore a basic element of well-being (Seligman, Ernst, Gillham, Reivich, & Linkins, 2009).

Is it possible for a teacher to teach joy? Yes, I believe it is. If a teacher provides students with an experience of joy, the students know from that experience on what joy is. If the teacher not only provides joyful experiences but is able to clearly show what conditions produce experiences of joy, the child learns how to create those conditions on their own. They can then find their way back to the sweet nectar of joy again and again. Relating this to cooperative games, we know that playing lovingly and cooperatively with friends is a joyful experience. Further, it is quite clear that the playful activity is the source of that joy. The child thus learns how to create joy—by simply playing kindly and cooperatively with friends. Being a teacher of joy, then, means providing experiences of joy through empowering pedagogies such as cooperative games!

CHAPTER SUMMARY

Young children do not need to be taught how to play. It is a natural expression of their health, well-being, and need to grow. Play can be categorized into a dozen or so common types, including sociodramatic play, imaginary play, rough-and-tumble play, and more. Most of these common types of play do not necessarily involve competition.

The term *cooperative play* was introduced to the social sciences by psychologist Mildred Parten in 1932. In Parten's theory of play stages, cooperative play represents the final stage of a progression of stages of play that children pass through as they develop socially. During the cooperative play phase, children learn how to coordinate with other children in meaningful ways. Social maturation is not complete without learning the lessons of cooperative play.

While noncompetitive play clearly is important to child development, the role of competitive play is much less clear. Indeed, the theory and scholarship presented in this book suggests that competitive play carries significant risks for children's wellbeing and development.

Facilitating cooperative play and games can be as simple as allowing free play, because children quite naturally play cooperatively on their own.

However, numerous educational purposes can be fulfilled by teaching with cooperative games in a more deliberate way.

Practice guidelines include providing developmentally appropriate cooperative play options. Children of age 3 or so who are in the associative play stage can contribute to imaginary collaborative projects, for example by adding ingredients to an imaginary bowl of soup or building a tower from blocks. Once children reach the cooperative play stage—typically between ages 4 and 6—they are ready for formal games with rules, such as cooperative board games and circle games. Additional guidelines for keeping the games inclusive, for using them to teach academic subjects, for SEL, and trauma-sensitive practice are provided in the chapter.

PLAY TO LEARN—TRY THIS!

HOW WOULD YOU FEEL?

This game *can be adapted for all ages.* It takes about 15 minutes to play. The SEL goals are to understand one's own emotions, recognize multiple perspectives, empathize, and ultimately to find common ground.

Directions:

Explain to the children that you are going to describe a situation to them and they will describe how they would feel. Ask, "How would you feel if . . . ?" and give them a series of different situations, such as the ones given below. If the children have different responses, point out that different people sometimes feel differently about the same thing. Then, as a group, see if you can come up with a situation that everyone feels the same about.

The following situations are likely to elicit different feelings:

How would you feel if . . .

> You looked up at the sky and there was a great big unicorn in it?
> You were given broccoli for lunch?
> You were asked to go on a roller coaster?
> You got to ride in a rocket to the moon?

The following situations are likely to elicit similar feelings:

How would you feel if . . .

> Someone grabbed the toy you were playing with?
> Someone said your shoes are ugly?

Your best friend moved away?
Your mother said she loves you?
You got a new puppy?

Variations:

Have children make faces rather than call out words. Or ask the children to volunteer the situations. If you like to draw, you can even draw faces on the chalkboard such as those shown in Figure 9.1 and have students name the emotions that they illustrate.

Figure 9.1. How Would You Feel? is an excellent game that builds social-emotional awareness in young children.

Putting It All Together:
A Pedagogy of Cooperative Games

As we reach the end of this book, we take a look at cooperative games from the long view. I will summarize and organize the theory, applications, methodology, and research to form a pedagogical framework. I hope it will provide you with a clear overall picture of the approach that you can carry with you in your teaching tool kit.

ELEMENTS OF THE PEDAGOGICAL FRAMEWORK

To articulate a pedagogical framework, we need to state: (1) theoretical underpinnings that justify using cooperative games in education, (2) a list of possible applications for the games, (3) methods and strategies, and (4) evidence to show that the methods are workable and effective in the real world.

Do you see the general outline of a pedagogical framework in what you have learned about cooperative games in this book? The necessary elements are there if you look. Let's bring them forward, summarize them, and connect them as a whole.

Supporting Theory

The theory of cooperative games is a montage of ideas from other theories put together in a new way. Here are the essential theories, by category and the individuals who developed them. Chapter references indicate the primary place in this book where they are discussed.

1. Theories of play in learning relevant to cooperative games in education
    Fundamental significance of play—Froebel (Chapter 1)
    Theories of cognitive development—Piaget (Chapter 1)
    Social-historical theory—Vygotsky (Chapter 1)
    Theory of experiential education—Dewey (Chapter 1)
    Theory of peace education—Montessori (Chapter 1)

Theory of Play Stages—Parten (Chapter 9)
Theory of cooperative games—Lentz & Cornelius; Orlick;
   Deacove (Chapter 1)
2. Theories of cooperation relevant to cooperative games in education
   Theory of social interdependence—Deutsch (Chapter 2)
   Realistic conflict theory—Sherif (Chapter 8)
   Social identity theory—Tajfel & Turner (Chapter 8)
   Theory of contact conditions, including superordinate goals
      (Chapter 8)
   Cooperative learning pedagogy (Chapter 6)
3. Theory of moral education relevant to cooperative games in education
   Caring theory—Noddings (Chapter 7)

Curriculum Applications

The educational applications and goals of cooperative games, as discussed in this book, include the following:

- Providing cooperation training to support academic cooperative learning
- Giving students an experience of welcoming and inclusion as an SEL "signature practice" as described by CASEL
- Addressing the SEL core competency of relationship skills as described by CASEL
- Preventing aggression in prosocially deficient youth by teaching them new norms and skills
- Promoting constructive contact among adversarial groups through superordinate goals and other conditions of constructive contact
- Reducing aggression related to social divisions and ethnocentrism
- Preventing bullying by nurturing a positive classroom climate
- Spurring critical examination of competition so that teachers and students can respond intentionally to its rarely discussed hazards
- Promoting inclusive education by setting new norms of cooperation and inclusivity as well as through positive personal experiences
- Providing moral education by nurturing experiences of caring
- Providing trauma-sensitive education through experiences of relational safety
- Teaching academic subjects to young children through developmentally appropriate play-based education within a guided play format
- Providing an alternative to screen-based entertainment
- Providing an experience of joy and hope
- Fostering the development of the whole child—cognitive, social, emotional, physical, and spiritual

- Teaching students values and skills of cooperation for the purpose of sustaining a healthy democracy
- Teaching cooperation to model group problem-solving and collective action to address shared problems at all scales up to and including global crises such as climate change and pandemics
- Teaching students how to use cooperation to nurture peace in communities of every scale, including local, national, and global

Methods and Strategies

Not all nominally "cooperative games" are of equal quality, nor are they all equally suitable for the classroom. For good results, you need to choose cooperative games that are designed well and that work in educational settings. In addition, your teaching methods and your facilitation skills affect what the educational impact of the games will be. Methods and strategies for choosing appropriate games and using them successfully include the following. These are discussed in greater detail earlier in this book, especially in Chapters 4 and 5.

- Choose cooperative games that correspond to the developmental stages that your students are in. Games that require strategy and that facilitate meaningful discussion are good for high-schoolers. Cooperative online games are an option after school. Middle schoolers benefit from big, inclusive group games. Older elementary schoolchildren like board games, active cooperative games on the playground, and cooperative activities such as painting murals and performing in skits. Primary school children enjoy simple board games, group games, and educational games. Pre-K and kindergarten students benefit from group games and cooperative free play activities—especially sociodramatic play. Children younger than preschool like gentle games and cooperative activities that adults initiate such as playing peekaboo, pat-a-cake, and chasing and hiding games.
- To evaluate cooperative games, and to design good games yourself, remember Orlick's four qualities of well-designed cooperative games: cooperation, inclusivity, acceptance, and fun.
- Choose games that reflect diverse cultures for multicultural education or games that appear culturally neutral/intersectional to promote inclusivity and diminish social divisions.
- Use cooperative games to improve classroom climate by integrating them across the curriculum for academic learning.
- Use cooperative games with Bandura's (1969) Five Principles of Social Change in the context of a cooperative training program to support cooperative learning.

- Use postgame reflection for group processing, getting feedback for next time, and, most important, helping students articulate lessons learned about cooperation.
- Use cooperative games at the start of class as a signature practice for welcoming and inclusion, as recommended by CASEL.
- Use the cooperative games employed in the Bay-Hinitz et al. (1994) study as a model for bullying prevention.
- Use cooperative games as an intervention for youth with chronic prosocial deficiencies as discussed by the Prepare Curriculum (Goldstein, 1999).
- Use methods outlined in the Contact Hypothesis (Allport, 1954) with cooperative games to bring adversarial social groups together.
- Run cooperative games during recess.
- Hold schoolwide "Cooperative Play Days" where students in all classes participate in cooperative games throughout the day.
- Set up cooperative board games in a gallery format so students can move from one game to another.
- Teach students how to make cooperative games using the guidelines in Chapter 5. Then, of course, play the games!

Evidence and Observations

Are you saying to yourself, "The theory of cooperative games sounds great, the intentions are noble, and there is some good research supporting it. But can they really make an impact in the complex world of today—and in *my* classroom?" To definitively answer this question, you need to try the games and see for yourself. Generate your own classroom-based research and learn from your own observations. The barrier to entry is low. Cooperative games are inexpensive or free, they can fit into any curriculum as a supplement, and they require little preparation on your part. It is true that more educational research is needed, but you—as a practitioner-scholar—can help rectify this deficit.

Try using cooperative games toward any of the many purposes discussed in this book. Share your findings and collaborate with colleagues to find new applications, methods, and strategies. The research discussed in this book, which shows that cooperative games teach cooperation and enhance prosocial behavior (Bay-Hinitz et al., 1994; Cohen, 1986; Goldstein, 1999, 2002; Orlick, 1981, 1983, 2006), and prevent aggression (Bay-Hinitz et al., 1994; Goldstein 1999, 2002) is clearly a strong foundation to stand on.

CONCLUSION

My intention in offering this pedagogical framework is not to box the practice in by stipulating what precisely is and isn't proper practice. No one is qualified to make rigid or blanket declarations about cooperative games. The cooperative games movement evolved as an inclusive and decentralized group effort—a folk movement with an idealistic spirit. It is open to all, malleable, and organic. Its brilliance lies in its recognition of the enormous social value of simply playing together, rather than against each other. This principle can doubtless be applied in countless ways yet to be discovered.

It is really very important for educators to understand the basic rationale and benefits of cooperative games. People learn through play. This makes cooperative games a powerful way to teach cooperation. Cooperation is key to happiness, peace, problem-solving, and productivity at all levels of social organization, from the classroom to the nation and even to the world as one giant global community. And so cooperative games fit into the big picture of all that we care about in a very natural yet profound way. Truly, we can play our way to a better world!

Figure E.1. Balancing Activities is a simple cooperative game in which players balance objects between themselves without using their hands. Directions are given in Chapter 4. Cooperative games such as this are a valuable classroom practice that teaches the vital skill and mindset of cooperation.

Answers to Questions for Reflection

CHAPTER 1. WHAT ARE COOPERATIVE PLAY AND GAMES?

1. No, he is not playing. For Henry, football is not pleasant or voluntary, so it does not fit the definition of play.
2. No, she is not playing, because there is no imaginary aspect to her activity and what she is doing has consequences in the real world.
3. Yes, play is a subjective experience, in part because it depends on the player's perception of pleasure.
4. Cooperative games have diverse benefits. No known single theory is comprehensive enough to encompass them all.
5. No, the child is playing alone. This is solitary play. Cooperative play occurs between real people, though a digital interface is sometimes present.

CHAPTER 2. LEARNING TO COOPERATE

1. Answers will vary.
2. Answers will vary.
3. Competitive sports involve cooperation within a team, but competition between teams. When groups compete against one another, they engage in intergroup competition.
4. Yes, indeed, lack of cooperation between social groups is a big problem for peace. As you will learn in Chapter 8, intergroup competition is the ultimate source of intergroup resentment, hostility, and aggression up to and including war, according to realistic conflict theory and social identity theory.
5. Cooperative games omit the us-versus-them dynamic whereby groups struggle against each other to win. Everyone is on the same team with one goal.

CHAPTER 3. RETHINKING COMPETITION

1. All answers are acceptable. The purpose of the questions is to prompt you to reflect and hypothesize. In fact, a competitive attitude as correlated to diminished academic achievement is discussed later in the chapter.
2. All answers are acceptable.
3. A possible example of antisocial fun or entertainment is the infamous gladiator games of Ancient Rome. Antisocial humor includes mean-spirited, racist, and sexist jokes.
4. Cooperative Tic-Tac-Toe and many other cooperative games mentioned in this book are examples of challenging games. Competition is not essential to challenge in games.

CHAPTER 4. A GALLERY OF COOPERATIVE GAMES

1. Answers will vary.
2. Cooperatively structured games are probably as ancient and universal as play itself. However, what we call "cooperative games" are games that are purposely designed as an alternative to competition. London Bridge Is Falling Down is a traditional cooperative game. No-Elimination Simon Says and Balloon Bop are modern cooperative games.
3. Answers will vary. For example, the cards could list days of the week or months of the year. Players scramble to line up in the proper sequence.

CHAPTER 5. A GUIDE TO FACILITATING COOPERATIVE GAMES

1. Answers will vary, but all games should reflect knowledge of the kinds of games that are appropriate for each developmental level.
2. Answers will vary but should include one open-ended question, one feeling question, one judgment question, one philosophical question, and one closing question.
3. Answers will vary. Extra kudos for answers that involve game testing and revision!

CHAPTER 6. COOPERATIVE GAMES TO SUPPORT COOPERATIVE LEARNING

1. Agree. Social interdependence theory shows that cooperation leads to better goal attainment than competition. This contradicts the Social Darwinist idea that competition breeds productivity. Likewise, social interdependence theory shows that progress is more likely to be the

fruit of cooperative than individualistic behavior, and that cooperation nurtures mental health. This undercuts the conceptions that exceptional individuals acting alone produce the triumphs of history and "rugged individualism" forges character.

2. Any three of the behaviors listed under the Learning Centers heading in Table 6.1 is correct.

3. Step 4 of the cooperative training method involves Bandura's principles of social learning.

CHAPTER 7. COOPERATIVE GAMES AND THE "SOFT SKILLS"

1. Social interdependence theory predicts that cooperation in general facilitates positive relationships and induces prosocial behavior, in alignment with the definition of SEL.

2. Possible answers: Cooperative games (1) obviate the possibility of being labeled a "loser"; (2) increase prosocial behavior, thereby reducing the likelihood of hurtful social interactions; and (3) increase the sense of belonging that accompanies an inclusive classroom.

3. Answers will vary. Possible answer: In the game Trust Fall, players catch a volunteer to prevent him from falling. If a player can observe her own emotions, she is likely to realize that she feels a sense of caring and responsibility as she catches her falling classmate.

CHAPTER 8. COOPERATIVE GAMES TO PREVENT AGGRESSION

1. Competition arouses the perception of group threat because it introduces the real possibility of relative loss. The sense of threat gives rise to intergroup bias. Hostility and escalating levels of aggression may ensue, depending on the particulars of the setting and individuals involved.

2. Social groups compete for top position in a social hierarchy relative to out-groups because it gives them self-esteem.

3. Accept all reasonable answers.

4. Answers will vary. The superordinate goal is usually the object of the game.

5. True. At its core, it is really that simple.

CHAPTER 9. COOPERATIVE GAMES IN EARLY CHILDHOOD EDUCATION

1. Possible answer: Encourage children to focus on the concept of personal best. In this way, children appreciate their partners for helping them measure their own performance.

2. Parallel play.
3. Parten's definition includes competitive play as a form of cooperative play.
4. The social effects are very different from one another. Teachers need to understand the differences so that they avoid unintended consequences when planning their play-based curricula.

Resources for Further Exploration

BOOKS

Caring: A Feminine Approach to Ethics and Moral Education by Nel Noddings. (1984). University of California Press.
No Contest: The Case Against Competition by Alfie Kohn. (1992). Houghton Mifflin.
Cooperative Games and Sports: Joyful Activities for Everyone, 2nd Edition by Terry Orlick. (2006). Human Kinetics.
Designing Groupwork: Strategies for the Heterogeneous Classroom, 3rd Edition by Elizabeth Cohen and Rachel Lotan. (2014). Teachers College Press.
Learning Together and Alone: Cooperative, Competitive, and Individualistic Learning, 3rd Edition by David W. Johnson & Roger T. Johnson. (1991). Prentice Hall.
Meeples Together: How and Why Cooperative Board Games Work by Christopher Allen and Shannon Appelcline. (2020). Gameplaywright.
The Cooperative Games Bullying Prevention Program by Suzanne Lyons. (2015). Child and Nature LLC.
The Prepare Curriculum: Teaching Prosocial Competencies, Revised Edition by Arnold P. Goldstein. (1998). Research Press.
The Psychology of Group Aggression by Arnold P. Goldstein. (2002). John Wiley & Sons, Ltd.

WEBSITES

CooperativeGames.com—Suzanne Lyons's website, a clearinghouse for cooperative games, especially as related to education. The site is also a source of cooperative games, books related to cooperative play, and professional development for teachers.
DEY.org—https://dey.org—the website for Defending the Early Years, an advocacy group founded by education professors Diane Levin and Nancy Carlsson-Paige. Its mission is to mobilize the early childhood education community to protect developmentally appropriate, play-based educational practices in early childhood classrooms.
EarthGames.nl—Anne Mijke van Harten's website, a panoply of products and a storehouse of practical information on cooperative games. It is also a supplier of play resources and products that connect people with

nature. Anne Mijke works with schools, too. She is an inspirational leader in the world of cooperative games.

FamilyPastimes.com—https://familypastimes.com—Jim Deacove's website. Jim is a founding father of the cooperative games movement. His company, *Family Pastimes*, is the world's first manufacturer of cooperative board games. His games are gentle and insightful and, many would say, display a touch of genius.

Peace Educators Allied for Children Everywhere (P.E.A.C.E)—https://peaceeducators.org. The website for P.E.A.C.E. is a good point of entry for educators and others who want to contribute to peace in the world through educational programs and methods that can be used in everyday life. A good source of information and a caring community of educators who work for peace.

SunnyGames—https://sunnygames.eu—the website of an independent European cooperative games publisher and distributor of cooperative games notable for the many fun and gentle cooperative games they supply to schools and homes across Europe.

References

Allen, C., & Appelcline, S. (2018). *Meeples together, how and why cooperative board games work*. Gameplaywright.

Allport, G. W. (1954). *The nature of prejudice*. Perseus Books.

American Psychological Association. (2020). *APA dictionary of psychology*. https://dictionary.apa.org

Bandura, A. (1969). *Principles of behavior modification*. Holt, Rinehart, and Winston.

Bandura, A. (1983). Psychological mechanisms of aggression. In R. G. Green & E. Donnerstein (Eds.), *Theoretical and empirical reviews* (pp. 1–40). Academic Press.

Bay-Hinitz, A. K. (2001). Prescribing games to reduce aggression in children. In C. E. Schaefer & S. E. Reid (Eds.), *Game play: Therapeutic use of childhood games* (2nd ed., pp. 336–383). John Wiley & Sons.

Bay-Hinitz, A. K., Peterson, R. F., & Quilitch, R. H. (1994). Cooperative games: A way to modify aggressive and cooperative behaviors in young children. *Journal of Applied Behavior Analysis, 27*(3), 435–446. https://doi.org/10.1901/jaba.1994.27-435

Ben-Ze'ev, A. (1990). Envy and jealousy. *Canadian Journal of Philosophy, 20*(4), 487–516. https://doi.org/10.1080/00455091.1990.10716502

Bickmore, K. (2011). Policies and program for safer schools: Are anti-bullying approaches impeding education for peace building? *Educational Policy, 25*(4), 648–687.

Boekaerts, M. (2002). Educational practice series, number 10, motivation to learn. International Bureau of Education, Publications Unit. https://www.iaoed.org/downloads/prac10e.pdf

Bruneau, E. G., Cikara, M., & Saxe, R. (2017). Parochial empathy predicts reduced altruism and the endorsement of passive harm. *Social Psychological and Personality Science, 8*(8), 934–942. https://doi.org/10.1177/1948550617693064

Burns, S. M., &Brainerd, C. J. (1979). Effects of constructive and dramatic play on perspective-taking in very young children. *Developmental Psychology, 15*, 512–521.

California Department of Education. (2013). *California preschool curriculum framework, Volume 3*. https://www.cde.ca.gov/sp/cd/re/documents/preschoolframeworkvol3.pdf

Carlsson-Paige, N. (2018, November). *Young children in the digital age: A parent's guide*. https://dey.org/wp-content/uploads/2018/11/young_children_in_the_digital_age_final_final.pdf

Cohen, E. G. (1986). *Designing groupwork: Strategies for the heterogeneous class-room*. Teachers College Press.

Cohen, E. G., & Lotan, R. A. (2014). *Designing groupwork: Strategies for the heterogeneous classroom* (3rd ed.). Teachers College Press.

Cohen-Charash, Y. (2009). Episodic envy. *Journal of Applied Social Psychology, 39*(9), 2128–2173. https://doi.org/10.1111/j.1559-1816.2009.00519.x

Coleman, P. T. (2017). World peace: How do we keep nations from nuclear war? *Psychology Today.* https://www.psychologytoday.com/us/blog/the-five-percent/201708/world-peace-how-do-we-keep-nations-thermonuclear-war

Collaborative for Academic, Social, and Emotional Learning (CASEL). (2019). *Social emotional learning, 3 signature practices playbook, a tool that supports systemic social and emotional learning.* https://schoolguide.casel.org/uploads/2018/12/CASEL_SEL-3-Signature-Practices-Playbook-V3.pdf

Collaborative for Academic, Social, and Emotional Learning (CASEL). (2020a). *About CASEL: History.* https://casel.org/history/

Collaborative for Academic, Social, and Emotional Learning (CASEL). (2020b). *CASEL's SEL framework. https://casel.org/fundamentals-of-sel/what-is-the-casel-framework/#relationship*

Copeland, W. E., Keeler, G., Angold, A., & Costello, E. J. (2007). Traumatic events and posttraumatic stress in childhood. *Archives of General Psychiatry, 64*(5), 577–584.

Cornelius, R. & Lentz, T. (1950). *All together: A manual of cooperative games* [Photocopy]. Attitude Research Laboratory, Washington University, St. Louis, Missouri.

Cornell, J. (1998). *Sharing nature with children, 20th anniversary edition.* Dawn Publications.

Deacove, J. (2021, January 21). Private interview with Suzanne Lyons.

Deci, E. L, Betley, G., Kahle, J., Abrams, L., & Porac, J. (1981). When trying to win: Competition or intrinsic motivation. *Personality and Social Psychology Bulletin, 7*(1), 79–83. https://doi.org/10.1177/014616728171012

Dennis, L. (1970). Play in Dewey's theory of education. *Young Children, 25*(4), 230-235. http://www.jstor.org/stable/42643331

Deranja, M. N. (2004). *For goodness' sake: Supporting children and teens in discovering life's highest values.* Crystal Clarity Publishers.

Deutsch, M. (1949a). A theory of co-operation and competition. *Human Relations, 2*(2), 129–152. https://doi.org/10.1177/001872674900200204

Deutsch, M. (1949b). An experimental study of the effects of cooperation and competition upon group process. *Human Relation,s 2*(3), 199–231. https://doi.org/10.1177/001872674900200301

Deutsch, M. (1985). *Distributive justice: A social-psychological perspective.* Yale University Press.

Dewey, J. (1916). *Democracy and education.* Project Gutenberg. https://www.gutenberg.org/files/852/852-h/852-h.htm

Duckworth, C. (2006). Teaching peace: A dialogue on Maria Montessori. *Journal of Peace Education, 39*(53).

Edutopia. (2011, October 6). *Social and emotional learning: A short history.* https://www.edutopia.org/social-emotional-learning-history

Edwards, V. B. (2017). *Putting it all together.* Aspen Institute, National Commission on Social, Emotional, and Academic Development. https://www.aspeninstitute.org/publications/putting-it-all-together/

Federal Trade Commission. (2020). *Monopolization defined.* https://www.ftc.gov/tips-advice/competition-guidance/guide-antitrust-laws/single-firm-conduct/monopolization-defined

Fletcher, A. & Kunst, K. (2006). *Guide to cooperative games for social change.* Common Action.

Forbs, H. D. (1997). *Ethnic conflict: Commerce, culture, and the contact hypothesis.* Yale University Press.

Forsyth, D. (1983). *An introduction to group dynamics.* Brooks/Cole Publishing Company.

Froebel, F. (1899). *Pedagogics of the kindergarten.* D. Appleton and Company. https://www.google.com/books/edition/Friedrich_Froebel_s_Pedagogics_of_the_Ki/KpUWAAAAIAAJ?hl=en&gbpv=1&printsec=frontcover

Froebel USA. (2019). *A brief history of kindergarten.* (2019). https://www.froebelgifts.com/history.htm

Garcia, S. M., Tor, A., & Schiff, T. M. (2013). The psychology of competition: A social comparison perspective. *Perspectives on Psychological Science, 8*(6), 634–650. https://doi.org/10.1177/1745691613504114

Gaskill, R. L., & Perry, B. D. (2014). The neurobiological power of play. In C. A. Malchiodi & D. A. Crenshaw (Eds.), *Creative arts and play therapy for attachment problems* (pp. 178–194). The Guildford Press.

Gilbert, P., McEwan, K., Bellew, R., Mills, A., & Gale, C. (2009). The dark side of competition: How competitive Behavior and striving to avoid inferiority are linked to depression, anxiety, stress, and self-harm. *Psychology and Psychotherapy, 82*(2), 123–126. https://doi.org/10.1348/147608308X379806

Goldstein, A. P. (1999). *The prepare curriculum: Teaching prosocial competencies.* Research Press.

Goldstein, A. P. (2002). *The psychology of group aggression.* John Wiley & Sons.

Goldstein, J. (2012). *Play in children's development and well-being.* Toy Institute of Europe. https://www.ornes.nl/wp-content/uploads/2010/08/Play-in-children-s-development-health-and-well-being-feb-2012.pdf

Gray, P. (2008, November 19). The value of play I: The definition of play gives insights. *Psychology Today.* https://www.psychologytoday.com/us/blog/freedom-learn/200811/the-value-play-i-the-definition-play-gives-insights

Gray, P. (2013). *Free to learn: Why unleashing the instinct to play will make our children happier, more self-reliant, and better students for life.* Basic Books.

Harrison, M. (1975). *For the fun of it! Selected cooperative games for children and adults.* Philadelphia Yearly Meeting.

Hartley, R. E., Frank, L. K., & Goldenson, R. M. (1952). *Understanding children's play.* Columbia University Press.

Hildebrand, D. (2018). John Dewey. *The Stanford encyclopedia of philosophy.* https://plato.stanford.edu/entries/dewey/

Hughes, B. (2002). *A playworker's taxonomy of play types* (2nd ed). London.

Hughes, F. (2010). *Children, play, and development.* Sage Publications.

Johnson, D. W., & Johnson, R. (1989). *Cooperation and competition: Theory and research*. Interaction Book Company.

Johnson, D. W., & Johnson, R. T. (1991). *Learning together and alone* (3rd ed.). Prentice Hall.

Johnson, D. W., & Johnson, R. (2005). New developments in social interdependence theory. *Psychology Monographs, 131*(4), 285–358.

Johnson, D. W., & Johnson, R. T. (2008). *The teacher's role in implementing cooperative learning*. Springer International Publications.

Johnson, D. W., & Johnson, R. T. (2011). Intellectual legacy: Cooperation and competition. In P. T. Coleman (Ed.), *Conflict, interdependence, and justice* (pp. 41–63). http://dx.doi.org/10.1007/978-1-4419-9994-8_3

Johnson, D. W., Johnson, R. T., Murayama, G., & Nelson, D. (1981). Effects of cooperative, competitive, and individualistic goal structures on achievement: A meta-analysis. *Psychological Bulletin, 89*(1), 47–62. https://doi.org/10.1037/0033-2909.89.1.47

Jones, S. M., & Kahn, J. (2017, September 13). *The evidence basis for how we learn: Supporting students' social, emotional, and academic development*. The Aspen Institute. https://assets.aspeninstitute.org/content/uploads/2017/09/SEAD-Research-Brief-9.12_updated-web.pdf

Katz, L. (2015). Lively minds: Distinctions between academic versus intellectual goals for young children. https://deyproject.wordpress.com/2015/04/09/lively-minds-distinctions-between-academic-versus-intellectual-goals-for-young-children/

Kohn, A. (1986). *No contest: The case against competition*. Houghton Mifflin Company.

Kohn, A. (2007). Who's cheating whom? *Phi Delta Kappan, 89*(2), 89–97.

Leacock, M. (2013). *Co-op interviews: Matt Leacock*. http://mechanics-and-meeples.com/2013/04/29/co-op-interviews-matt-leacock-pandemic/

Lents, N. (2017, May). Why play is important. Animal behavior helps illuminate why we play. *Psychology Today*. https://www.psychologytoday.com/us/blog/beastly-behavior/201705/why-play-is-important

Levi, D. (2007). *Group dynamics for teams* (2nd ed.) Sage Publications.

Levin, D. (2003, March). *Beyond banning war and superhero play: Meeting children's needs in violent times*. https://commercialfreechildhood.org/wp-content/uploads/archive/levin_warplay.pdf

Levin, D. (2010). Remote control childhood: Combating the hazards of media culture in school. *New Horizons in Education, 58*(3), 14–25. https://files.eric.ed.gov/fulltext/EJ966656.pdf

Lilley, I. (1967). *Friedrich Froebel:, A selection from his writings*. Cambridge University Press.

Louv, R. (2008). *Last child in the woods*. Algonquin Books.

Lyons, S. (2015). *The cooperative games bullying prevention program: Cooperative games for a warm school climate, pre-K to grade 2*. Child and Nature LLC.

Lyons, S. (2021). Untitled, unpublished work.

Marean, C. W. (2015). The most invasive species of all. *Scientific American, 313*(2), 33–39. https://doi.org/10.1038/scientificamerican0815-32

May, R. (1977). *Anxiety in America*. W. W. Norton & Company.

McLeod, S. (2018). *The preoperational stage of cognitive development*. https://www.simplypsychology.org/preoperational.html

Mead, M. (1937). *Cooperation and competition among primitive peoples.* McGraw-Hill.

Montessori, M. (1912). *The Montessori method: Scientific pedagogy as applied to child education in "The Children's Houses," with additions and revisions by the author.* Frederick A. Stokes Company. http://digital.library.upenn.edu/women/montessori/method/method.html

Motyl, A. J. (2000). "Ethnocentrism." *Encyclopedia of Nationalism* (pp. 152–153). Elsevier.

Noddings, N. (1984). *Caring: A feminine approach to ethics and moral education.* University of California Press.

Norem-Hebeisen, A. A., & Johnson, D. W. (1981). The relationship between cooperative, competitive, and individualistic attitudes and differentiated aspects of self-esteem. *Journal of Personality, 49*(4), 415–426. https://doi.org/10.1111/j.1467-6494.1981.tb00223.x

Nowak, M. A. (2012). Why we help: The evolution of cooperation. *Scientific American, 307*(1), 34–39. https://doi.org/10.1038/scientificamericanhuman1112-92

Ogburn, W. F., & Nimkoff, M. F. (1958). *Sociology* (4th ed.). Houghton-Mifflin Company.

Orlick, T. D. (1978). *The cooperative sports and games book: Challenge without competition.* Human Kinetics.

Orlick, T. D. (1981). Positive socialization via cooperative games. *Developmental Psychology, 17*(4), 426–429. https://doi.org/10.1037/0012-1649.17.4.426

Orlick, T. (1982). *The second cooperative sports and games book.* Pantheon Books.

Orlick, T. (1983). Enhancing love and life mostly through play and games. *Journal of Humanistic Counseling, Education & Development, 21*(4), 153–164. https://doi.org/10.1002/j.2164-4683.1983.tb00228.x

Orlick, T. (2006). *Cooperative games and sports, Joyful activities for everyone* (2nd ed.). Human Kinetics.

Orlick, T. D., McNally, J., & O'Hara, T. (1978). *Cooperative games: Systematic analysis and cooperative impact.* Hemisphere Publishing Corporation.

Parten, M. (1932). Social participation among pre-school children. *Journal of Abnormal and Social Psychology, 27*(3), 243–269. https://doi.org/10.1037/h0074524

Passe, A. (2010). *A brief history of kindergarten.* https://www.redleafpress.org/assets/clientdocs/social_media/IsEverybodyReadyForKindergarten.pdf

Pawlo, E., Lorenzo, A., Eichert, B., & Ellis, M.J. (2019, October 28). All SEL should be trauma-informed. *Phi Delta Kappan, 101*(3), 37–41. https://kappanonline.org/all-sel-should-be-trauma-informed-schools-pawlo-lorenzo-eichert-elias76390-2/

Posselt, J. R., & Lipson, S. K. (2016). Competition, anxiety, and depression in the college classroom: variations by student identity and field of study. *Journal of College Student Development, 57*(8), 973–989. https://doi.org/10.1353/csd.2016.0094

Ramirez, J. M. (2003). Hormones and aggression in childhood and adolescence. *Aggression and Violent Behavior, 8*(6), 621–644. https://doi.org/10.1016/S1359-1789(02)00102-7

Ritsuko, R. (2021). The poetic mind, the key to creating hope and joy in education. In I. Nuñez, & J. Goulah (Eds.) *Hope and joy in education, engaging daisaku ikeda across curriculum and context.* Teachers College Press.

Rizzi, K. (2021, January 30). *Trauma informed practices for schools* [Workshop session]. California Association for the Education of Young Children (CAEYC) Workshop.

Rosenzweig, M. L. (2003). *Win-win ecology: How the earth's species can thrive in the midst of human enterprise.* Oxford University Press.

Sapon-Shevin, M. (2007). *Widening the circle: The power of inclusive classrooms.* Beacon Press.

Schmuck, R. (1985). Learning to cooperate, cooperating to learn: Basic concepts. In R. Slavin, S. Sharan, S. Kagan, R. Hertz-Lazarowitz, C. Webb, R. Schmuck, (Eds.), *Learning to cooperate, cooperating to learn* (pp. 1–4). Plenum.

Seligman, M. E. P., Ernst, R. M., Gillham, J., Reivich, K., & Linkins, M. (2009). *Positive education: Positive psychology and classroom interventions,* Oxford Review of Education, 35(3), 293–311. https://www.aps.sg/files/GELC%202014 /Pre-reading%20Articles/Keynote_5_Boniwell_Seligmans_Positive_Education .pdf

Sherif, M. (1958). Superordinate goals in the reduction of intergroup conflict. *American Journal of Sociology, 63*(4), 349–356. http://www.jstor.org/stable/2774135

Shindler, J. (2017). Examining the use of competition in the classroom. In *Transformative classroom management.* (2009). John Wiley & Sons. http://web.calstatela .edu/faculty/jshindl/cm/Chapter18competition-final.htm

Sidanius, J., & Pratto, F. (1999). *Social dominance: An intergroup theory of social hierarchy and oppression.* Cambridge University Press.

Singer, D. G, Michnick Golinkoff, R., & Hirsh-Pasek, K. (2006). *Play=Learning: How play motivates and enhances children's cognitive and social-emotional growth.* Oxford University Press.

Stallen, M., Griffioen, N., & Sanfey, A. (2017). Why are we not more selfish? What the study of brain and behavior can tell us. *Frontiers in Young Minds, 5*(47). https://doi.org/10.3389/frym.2017.00047

Stuart, K. (2019, May 19). Minecraft at 10: A decade of building things and changing lives. *The Guardian.* https://www.theguardian.com/games/2019/may/18/mine craft-at-10-building-things-and-changing-lives

Sumner, W. G. (1906). *Folkway:, A study of the sociological importance of usages, manners, customs, mores, and morals.* Ginn & Company.

Tajfel, H., & Turner, J. C. (1986). The social identity theory of group behavior. In S. Worchel & W. G. Austin (Eds.), *The psychology of intergroup relations* (pp. 7–24). Burnham Inc. Pub.

Thompson, C. (2016, April 14). The Minecraft generation: How a clunky Swedish computer game is teaching millions of children to master the digital world. *The New York Times.* https://www.nytimes.com/2016/04/17/magazine/the-minecraft -generation.html

Tomasello, M. (2009). *Why we cooperate.* MIT Press.

Toub, T. S., Rajan, V., Golinkoff, R. M., & Hirsh-Pasek, K. (2016). Guided play: A solution to the play versus discovery learning dichotomy. In D. C. Geary & D. B. Berch (Eds.), *Evolutionary psychology: Evolutionary perspectives on child development and education* (pp. 117–141). Springer International Publishing. https://doi.org/10.1007/978-3-319-29986-0_5

Tovey, H. (2020). *Froebel's principles and practice today.* https://www.froebel.org .uk/training-and-resources/pamphlets

Toy Association. (2020). *U.S. sales data.* http://www.toyassociation.org/ta/about-us /board/toys/about-us/board-of-directors.aspx?hkey=c9f4df92-83c6-4d6a-b19a -4ec4d184f1ff

Turner, F. (2006). Why study new games? *Games and Culture, 1*(1), 1–4. https://doi .org/10.1177/1555412005281823

Turner, J. C. (1981). The experimental social psychology of intergroup behavior. In J. C. Turner & H. Giles (Eds.), *Intergroup behavior* (pp. X). University of Chicago Press.

United Nations Office of the High Commissioner on Human Rights. (1989). *Convention on the rights of the child.* https://www.ohchr.org/en/professionalinterest /pages/crc.aspx

University of Rochester Medical Center. (2020). Kids' headaches: The diagnosis is difficult. *Health Encyclopedia.* https://www.urmc.rochester.edu/encyclopedia /content.aspx?contenttypeid=1&contentid=615

U.S. Department of Health and Human Services. (n.d.). *What is bullying?* https:// www.stopbullying.gov

Vygotsky, L. S. (1929). The problem of the cultural development of the child II. *Journal of Genetic Psychology, 36,* 415–432. https://www.marxists.org/archive /vygotsky/works/1929/cultural_development.htm

Vygotsky, L. S. (1930). *Mind and society.* Harvard University Press.

Weingartner, S., & Stahel, L. (2019). Online aggression from a sociological perspective: An integrative view on determinants and possible countermeasures. *The Association for Computational Linguistics (ACL), Third Workshop on Abusive Language Online, Proceedings of the Workshop.* https://www.aclweb.org /anthology/volumes/W19-35/

White, R. (n.d.). *The power of play: A research summary on play and learning.* https://www.childrensmuseums.org/images/MCMResearchSummary.pdf

Williams, M. K. (2017). John Dewey in the 21st century. *Journal of Inquiry & Action in Education, 9*(1), 91–102. https://digitalcommons.buffalostate.edu/jiae /vol9/iss1/7/

Wood, K. C., Smith, H., & Grossniklaus, D. (2001). Piaget's stages of development. In M. Orey (Ed.), *Emerging perspectives on learning, teaching, and technology* (p. X). http://projects.coe.uga.edu/

Yang, L. 2017. *Awakening together.* Wisdom Publications.

Zastrow, C. (2009). *Social work with groups: A comprehensive workbook.* Brooks/ Cole Cengage Learning.

Zigler, E. F., & Bishop-Josef, S. A. (2006). The cognitive child versus the whole child: Lessons from 40 years of Head Start. In Singer, D., R. Michnick Golinkoff, & K. Hirrsch-Pasek (Eds.), *Play equals learning* (pp. 15–35). Oxford University Press.

Index

Note: *Italicized* page numbers indicate directions for specific cooperative games.

About the Author

Suzanne Lyons is a former physics and general science teacher, a teacher trainer, an author, an illustrator, and a game designer. Her degrees are in physics (University of California, Berkeley), earth science (M.A., Sacramento State University), and education (M.A., Stanford University), and she holds a California teaching credential. She specializes in science education and social-emotional learning.

Suzanne's background in science education includes teaching honors physics and general science at Mountain View High School in California. She is also the author or co-author of over 40 books that teach science. This includes her role as co-author of the college-level textbook program Conceptual Integrated Science, which is published by Pearson Education and is now in its 3rd edition.

Suzanne's work in social-emotional learning centers on cooperative games. She founded the website and small business CoopertiveGames.com in 2009. In 2015, she self-published *The Cooperative Games Bullying Prevention Program*. In 2018, she published The Baby Beluga Game, a cooperative board game that she created in collaboration with the singer Raffi. The Baby Beluga Game, which teaches both STEM and SEL, won two Dr. Toy Awards and a Parents' Choice Award in 2018. Currently, Suzanne provides workshops and conference presentations on cooperative games and continues to educate the public through her website, CooperativeGames.com.

Printed and bound by CPI Group (UK) Ltd, Croydon, CR0 4YY

09/06/2025

14685970-0002